Tomatomania!

Tomatomania!

*A Fresh Approach to Celebrating Tomatoes
in the Garden and in the Kitchen*

Scott Daigre & Jenn Garbee

PHOTOGRAPHS BY STACI VALENTINE

ST. MARTIN'S GRIFFIN
NEW YORK

All recipe photographs and photographs on pages v, vi, vii, x, 3, 5, 23, 27, 32, 48, 63, 64, 67, 76, 78, 79, 80, 83, 98, 100, 115, 116, 117, 121, 126, 134, 135, 137, and 141 are copyright © Staci Valentine 2015.

Photographs on pages xiii, 6–7, 8, 9, 11, 14, 16, 17, 20, 24, 29, 38, 41, 44–45, 47 (L), 48, 52, 71, 72, 74, 77, 81, 86, 87, 89, 91, 93, 94, 96, 101, 110, 113, 114, 122–23, 138, 142, and 189 are courtesy of Scott Daigre.

Photographs on pages 21, 25, 26, 31, 34, 35, 36, 42, 47 (A–K), 49, 52, 57, 59, 60, 61, 63, 65, 103, 106, 107, 119, 125, 143, 190, 191, 193, and 198 are courtesy of Sam Hamann.

Photographs on pages 51, 76, 78, 79, and 200 are courtesy of Trude Rutan.

Photograph on page xi is courtesy of John Daigre, Jr.

Photograph on page 37 is courtesy of Brad Gates.

Illustrations by Sam Hamann
Book Design by Rita Sowins / Sowins Design

www.stmartins.com

The Library of Congress Cataloging-in-Publication Data is available upon request.

ISBN 978-1-250-05728-0 (trade paperback)
ISBN 978-1-4668-6102-2 (e-book)

St. Martin's Griffin books may be purchased for educational, business, or promotional use. For information on bulk purchases, please contact Macmillan Corporate and Premium Sales Department at 1-800-221-7945, extension 5442, or write specialmarkets@macmillan.com.

First Edition: January 2015

10 9 8 7 6 5 4 3 2 1

For Noon and Nub,
and for Sam, the real gardener
in the family

Contents

Foreword

Gardening is not a rational act. –MARGARET ATWOOD

My father—who was not prone to aphorisms—once told me—"a man can truly be happy only if his hands are able to touch the soil." My mother, who routinely channeled Virginia Woolf, liked to say, "One cannot love or work with passion if one has not dined with equal passion."

Fast-forward forty years. I am a visiting chef in a public school helping thirty first-grade gardeners harvest zebra tomatoes, sugar snap peas, and multicolored carrots. A mosaic of ingredients hits the hot wok and I ask the kids what else we should add . . . ginger, garlic, fresh mint, chili? A chorus of enthusiastic voices squeals yes to each. We eat, perched on planter boxes, enjoying food that still glows of the garden. I ask if anyone is trying these vegetables for the first time and hands go up. One girl confesses her mom would be shocked—she normally didn't eat "anything green" at home.

I've come to expect small miracles like this in the garden and am reminded that lecturing kids about food choices cannot match their utter delight in growing and eating real food. Watch someone of any age taste their first homegrown tomato; it is a transformational moment, particularly after years of enduring what I call "zombie" tomatoes. Found year-round in the supermarket, zombies look just like real tomatoes . . . but aren't. These undead orbs stagger through people's meals, sucking the flavor out of everything in their path.

Take heart! The surest way to fight this zombie onslaught is through an irrational act of faith and defiance: namely, growing your own. *Tomatomania!* is the definitive guide for beginning one's own exciting tomato odyssey—from plant to plate and beyond. Because when eager gardeners commit to grow their own food, it is also a commitment to something deeper: a pledge to put their hands in the soil, to be truly happy, and to eat with passion.

—CHEF CLAUD MANN, HOST OF *DINNER & A MOVIE* ON TBS

Introduction

Stop! Don't buy your seedlings yet! I hope I caught you in time. I *know*. Waiting is hard. You can almost taste those summer tomatoes, can't you? If you got a little excited and already bought your seedlings, it's all good. No matter where you are in your season, I'm anxious to help you make the most of it.

I love tomatoes. Every color, every size, every wrinkled, striped, and flattened orb. When spring comes around, I can't think of anything else. I plant "rare" heirlooms first, then last year's best producers, my favorite cherries, and the hybrid workhorses that will be sure to fill the counter by harvest time. Then more of *all* of them.

Some of them will sit in the bed of my truck too long and get a bit leggy. But most will make it to the vegetable garden or into a lonely pot in need of a resident. Some may find themselves firmly rooted in that bare stretch near the garage, or maybe among the roses and shrubs in the perennial border. Soon, I'll have ten, maybe twenty seedlings. Okay, fifty. Know that feeling? If not, you may soon.

I can easily trace my tomato hysteria to my grandfather, Mom's dad. Pa Pa was the best kind of gardener. No offense to the zucchini and cucumbers, corn and lima beans, but to me, his garden was all about *tomatoes*. If I close my eyes, I can still smell his garden shed: a gumbo of Louisiana Delta soil and moisture and compost—with a little radical pesticide aroma mixed in for good measure.

[My first garden in Denver]

Liberal pesticide use wasn't the only thing that was different about growing tomatoes back then. Every year, with practiced and religious precision, Pa Pa grew rows and rows of Better Boys, a popular old-school hybrid. There was no sway there. **Bright red, perfectly round with a medium-large girth;** those were the qualities you looked for in a good tomato back then. Oh, and that taste! It was the taste that became *the* hallmark of summer. Remember those days? I still toss a few Better Boys into my garden every year.

To help you find the same success, though without pesticides and with a more open mind for tomato variety, we'll start by assessing your site and home garden. Is the soil prepped? Are your stakes, cages, and fertilizers all in line, ready to go? If you're a seasoned

Tomatomaniac, the answer will probably be a resounding *"Yes!"* (We tend to get a little excited about these things.)

If not, we'll get there after you **develop your tomato strategy.** (Yes, there really *is* such a thing!) If you first evaluate your growing conditions and develop your plan for the season, you'll make great strides toward that soon-to-be immensely successful summer tomato harvest. You will also make smarter and more appropriate choices when you shop for seedlings. My hope is that as we move into the growing season, I can charm you tomato veterans into trying new varieties, strategies, and practices that will make your efforts this season even more successful and rewarding.

First-timer? This is your year. We'll start with the basics. Take a deep breath. Growing tomatoes isn't difficult, time consuming, or physically taxing. The plant's practically a weed. But the rewards, oh, the rewards! Keep this book handy, and we'll plow through the season together. Soon, you'll be growing (and cooking!) better tomatoes than I do.

Enough talk. **Time to get our hands dirty.**

Almost. One more thing before we get started. Let's make this fun. I'm a hugely enthusiastic gardener, but I've been known to be a *lazy* one as well. I'd rather do just about anything than spend hours pinching tomatoes on a hot July afternoon. Perfection has never been my goal, and it needn't be yours. In these pages, if I do my job well, I will provide you with all the tools you need to succeed. Use them. And then step away from the "always perfect" gardening illusion and just relax. Let's all follow good gardening practices, but let's try not to be so *serious*. **Have** *fun*! Those plants will be just fine, better than fine, even if we don't fuss over them all day every day. And really, in today's online era, couldn't we all stand to have a little more backyard fun?

Tomatomania started in Southern California at an amazing nursery called Hortus over twenty years ago. Unbelievable. My unending thanks to all of you who have guided and supported us, hosted us, worked hard to make events happen, and have generally kept this crazy circus on its feet. It's been such a great ride, and there's so much more in store.

Welcome to Tomatomania! Caution: There is no cure.

[You never know what (or who) you'll find at a Tomatomania event!]

All Systems Go?

Considering your options and finding
the perfect spot for your garden

I s your garden tomato-ready? Lace up your boots! Let's get out there and find out. It's time to consider how your site, your soil, and the sun's path through your garden (some of which might have changed in recent seasons) affects your ability to grow tomatoes. Yep, time to think like a tomato plant.

First, I'll challenge you to choose the best site for your new garden, or your next garden, if you've grown tomatoes before. Look closely. What do you have to work with? What gets in the way? How can you use both to your advantage? Assessing your site is a crucial step toward a successful summer in the tomato garden.

After that, I'll help you decide how you want, or need, to grow your tomatoes. In the ground? Containers? Raised beds? Terraces? A hillside? What about hydroponics? (Sorry, that's a different book.) Maybe you have multiple spaces to plant, which is terrific. There are a lot of options to consider, and any of these methods can result in a great harvest.

And experienced growers, before you flip right past this chapter, let me ask you: Where will you plant your tomatoes this year? If you've grown tomatoes before—*especially* if you've grown tomatoes before—reassessing your environment can be a game changer.

Have those boots on yet?

⚜ OK, So You're a Farmer Now... ⚜

Well then, tomato farmer, let's start at the very beginning. Where will you plant your tomatoes? Simple enough question, right?

Faced with that question, many of you seasoned veterans will trot right out and point to your usual summer garden spot—the one now covered with weeds—and call it a day. But remember, just because that plot is the sunniest, or a safe distance from the trampoline, doesn't mean tomato plants are going to love it there again this season.

Let me ask you this: How was your harvest last year? How many years have you grown tomatoes in that space? It might be time for a change.

Sure, if you add compost like a fiend, thereby keeping the soil supremely active all year, you might be able to adequately rejuvenate the soil and reduce some of the lingering disease and pest problems that can challenge us in the growing season. But who does that, really? Be honest. If you've seen a decline in plant growth, vitality, and harvest amounts in the last few years, your best move toward a successful harvest this summer may be to, well, *move* it.

Do what farmers do: Rotate your crops. Prepare multiple spaces, or heck, multiple pots, that can host different combinations of vegetables in successive years. This is how you keep the soil healthy and grow terrific produce.

New tomato gardeners, you may not have to worry about this in your first season, but you'll want to pay attention to this concept in the future as you become hopelessly obsessed with growing home-grown tomatoes. Trust me on this one.

TOMATO GROWING 101:

Changing the location of your tomato garden from year to year is not only a good idea, it can be imperative if you want your plants to thrive and produce the kind of summer harvest we all dream about.

Rookie Luck It's true, beginner's luck happens in the vegetable garden as often as on the roulette table. Maybe you succeeded beyond your wildest imagination in that initial year, only to see your crops fail dismally in successive years as the plants fell prey to disease and pests. That's not so much a comment on your gardening skills as it is on the natural state of things, I promise.

Firstly, when you plant in the same space year after year, soils tire and nutritional value is reduced. You have to be really proactive and add a lot of new organic material each year to counteract that reality.

Secondly, diseases that tomatoes are prone to, such as wilt or blight, and the pests that love them (hornworms, tomato beetles, and other monsters) are also likely to set up housekeeping in that area. (Gardeners in warmer zones, this is why it helps to take your plants out and clean them up well in the fall/winter even though they'd often happily live through until the spring!) That growing population or concentration may cause your plants to die off earlier and earlier each season. It goes without saying that fruit production will be adversely affected.

Yes, some of us have neighbors, relatives, or friends who have gardened in the exact same place for over a decade with no decreasing returns. Don't you just hate that? They're very lucky tomato gardeners. If this is you, and you've yet to have an increase in disease problems, carry on. But as the season goes along, keep an eye out for signs of trouble that might hint at the need for a new space next year.

[Now THAT was a great first harvest!]

⁍ Find the Sweet Spot ⁍

Okay, but move or start the garden *where* exactly? We all have only a hundred square feet when we want a hundred acres, right? Tomatoes need sun—full sun— in order to be the most productive, healthy plants they can be. That's the cardinal rule of tomato placement. Find that spot.

In some established gardens, it could be as simple as moving from one corner of your veggie bed to another. Or, if you use multiple raised beds, planting your tomatoes in beds three and four instead of one and two. Just take a minute to look at the garden with a new set of eyes and evaluate the basics. I'm betting you can find another *sunny* option.

Case in point, when my partner, Sam, and I moved into our first home I planted tomatoes everywhere. *Everywhere*. Desperate to recruit more heirloom space, I even yanked up the concrete in the middle of the driveway to plant seedlings. (Don't believe a word Sam says; the neighbors were absolutely *thrilled*.)

But "full sun" doesn't mean tomatoes need hot sun *all day* long. Commercial tomatoes are a field crop, in the sun from dawn to dusk. The varieties that thrive in commercial fields have been bred for that. In our home gardens, most varieties will be quite happy with liberal amounts of sun, but it's not imperative to provide all-day exposure in order to have a successful season.

In fact, many varieties, especially heirlooms that come from more temperate parts of the world, may not like intense and constant sun exposure. Your plants are likely to look better, *and* produce tomatoes longer, if not completely sun-stressed every day of the season.

"Full sun" in homegrown tomato lingo actually means six to eight hours of uninterrupted sun a day. That's easier to find in your garden than twelve hours. It means that spot with morning and midday sun could be perfect. And the sunny hours don't need to be concurrent. Exposure from 8:00 A.M. until 11:00 A.M. and 2:00 A.M. until 6:00 A.M. qualifies just fine. If you get to make a choice between planting in a location with morning, midday, or late-afternoon sun, choose the warmest sunny stretch of the day.

When to Apply SUNscreen Part of the full-sun equation is that tomatoes want and need heat in order to grow and fruit successfully. That "warmest sun" concept is especially important if you happen to live in a more temperate zone with cool summers or widely variable summer temperatures.

But, if you live in an area known for excessive heat, you may actually be doing your plants a favor if they get a little shade (as long as they get the necessary sun exposure) during scorching midday hours.

[Jaune Flamme]

❧ Branching Out ❧

As you look for the *perfect* spot, here are a few other things to consider:

- Dig a little. Carry your shovel with you as you look for new tomato-growing opportunities. When you find a promising spot, try to dig a hole. If that soil is unyielding, rocky, all sand, or way too wet, you may want to scratch it off the list and move on.

- That six-foot tree you planted in the corner of the yard must be larger than it was last year, right? Consider that and all other potential shadow positions in high summer. Canyon walls, apartments next door, and that new play structure might all affect garden exposure and hours of direct sun. (And tree roots mean extra competition, too!)

- Reflected brightness and retained heat from a light-colored wall or fence can do wonders to increase the productivity of your season. Use that to your advantage.

- Where's the rain going? Did you change the garden grade when you put in that putting green or patio? Tree growth and other interruptions in sun exposure are generally easy to see and assess. Grade changes, not so much. Pay attention to where water gathers in a generous rainstorm or after a sprinkler soaking. That's not where you want your tomato garden to be.

- *Brrrrr!* If you have a large property or garden area, that wet area may also be the lowest place on your property, topographically speaking. That may also mean it is the coldest part of the garden—another reason to avoid the space.

- If you live in an area that gets liberal summer rain (and even if you don't), can you plant on a hill, berm, or even a slight slope of any kind? It doesn't have to be huge. Most of you have been hilling up rows in your garden since Mr. McGregor was a kid, right? Hillside or berm planting is especially beneficial for rainy areas because when it gets too wet, tomatoes get exactly what they want: sharp drainage. The first tomatoes ever found, the precursors of Tomatomania, are generally thought to have been found on a hillside in South America.

- Do you have a new backyard wind tunnel NASA doesn't know about? Be they winds that come "whippin' down the plain" or just a subtle ocean breeze, air movement cools things off. That's *not* your goal. Look for natural windbreaks and plant behind a garden shed, a thick row of hedges, or a sturdy fence. Or create your own temporary screen, just like you do when you go to the beach really early in the season. (You know this works.) You'll still get some beneficial air circulation but a screen will raise garden temperatures a good deal, and you'll see the proof when it's time to harvest.

- Did you rescue a puppy who likes to dig in the garden? Yes, even lifestyle changes can require you to move the garden or change your growing patterns.

Backyard Soul Searching If you're still perplexed, or if your garden, neighborhood, or even city is entirely new to you, why not ask a garden-friendly neighbor, area Master Gardener, landscape designer, or other expert to walk your garden with you, plot the sun's summer track, and identify opportunities and potential problems?

Or you can just do what my grandfather did and situate your veggies dead center in the backyard, away from trees, border plants, the house, and anything else that would block sun from those treasured tomato plants.

Decomp 101 Materials that once were living begin to decompose when left alone and allowed contact with air and some moisture. You know this; you watch crime dramas on TV, right? It's true. Compost happens. And it's a good thing to get started on now.

Yes, the percentages of nitrogen and carbon, your choice and size of materials, and even how wet the pile is (which affects oxygen content), are all important considerations if you need compost in less than thirty days. Do some homework and explore the process in more detail if that's your aim. There are plenty of online and nursery shop compost geeks (I was one) out there to help you.

Most of us have a different agenda: We simply want to make compost—whenever. It couldn't be easier. Pile up leaves, *light* garden trimmings (no, not huge thick stumps), *thin* layers of grass clippings (only *if* you are not using herbicides or insecticides on your lawn), and nongreasy kitchen and vegetable scraps. Cover the pile with a tarp or something similar if you need to keep critters out. That also prevents the pile from becoming too dried out or too wet, depending on where you live. Moisten as needed and turn the pile over (which is called aerating) when you think about it, every so often. You've just created a "cool pile," meaning a compost pile that will be ready . . . when it's ready. Like most things in life.

When the entire pile, or typically a center section, looks dark and soil-like, spread those parts out on top of your garden area or mix it right on in there. This is how you *amend* your soil, whether you make your own or buy a bagged or bulk product at a local nursery. In the garden, the definition is literal. You need to *change* your planting area for the better. Mission accomplished, for the moment at least. You need to do this more than once a year. Twice is good, four times is better, once a month is best, and you'll have a very happy garden.

Your best friend in pursuit of modern compost? A good old-fashioned bale of hay. Get one at a feed store near you. Add the hay, along with garden trimmings and other compostables, so that you can quickly add some bulk to the pile. Easy, right?

❧ Field Envy ❧

Unless you own a farm (or a private island some-where), space is almost always an issue when you are looking for new potential garden plots. So maybe you don't need to move your *entire* veggie garden. Tomatoes are more than happy to strike out on their own. What about the small, but sunny, space behind the garage, the patio outside the kitchen door, or the gravel area on the far side of the house? Leave the corn where it is. Consider creating your very own tomato annex.

If all this reaps no reward, there's always the "shared" space possibility for the summer season. Could you squeeze some tomatoes into the rose garden? Sneak them in while your partner (the rose lover) is out shopping. What about the intermittent spaces in perennial plantings (among the daylilies, irises, or lavender), or in borders where colorful annu-als like alyssum, sunflowers, and calendulas thrive each season? Those are probably planted in full sun and yes, your tomatoes could be happy there. Before all is lost, are you friendly with your neighbor who's got five hundred square feet of prime sunny space just across the fence? Hey, it's worth a shot.

[Chickens will eat up kitchen scraps (and tomatoes) faster than any compost pile.]

[For best results, look for a container
that won't heat up intensely and fry the
roots during the height of summer.]

Nothing? Then leave the soil in your current garden barren for a season or two. Or three. It's what you can do. Layer the entire existing garden with compost, leaves, hay, or other rich mulch—or a wonderful combo of all those organic ingredients. Lay it on thick, a good eight to ten inches.

Add some fertilizer to help activate the soil while it waits (patiently!) for future tomatoes. Plant this year's crop in containers or grow bags situated right on top of your current space. Do this for even a couple of seasons, and you'll address the tired or diseased soil question and hopefully create a new, vibrant garden in its place. I'll give you more hints on growing in containers next.

❧ Getting Potted ❧

Whether you're planting two dozen of your favorite heirlooms in pulp pots on top of last year's vegetable garden, or a single dependable hybrid in that French urn by the back door, you've made a good move. Sure, it's hard to beat Mother Earth. But there are a lot of reasons why container growing is a *great* idea.

For starters, pots are mobile, so it's possible to move them to where conditions are best as the season goes along and if the need arises. You also have the opportunity to (and must) create a perfect soil mix for your plants. You won't have either option in the garden. Other benefits include sharp drainage, which is almost assured.

And here's a biggie: Soil in a pot warms more quickly than in the ground. *Tomatoes in pots will generally ripen ten to fourteen days earlier than the same variety planted in the ground.* Do I need to repeat that one for you gardeners on the beach or the Canadian border? Growing in containers could be the key to a good season if your climate requires a quick turnaround.

So growing "in the box" is definitely not a lesser choice, just a different one. What makes a good container? Anything that holds soil and has a drain or drainage holes, for a start. With that as a guide, and adherence to just a few other rules, many things work well. We'll get into specific types of containers later, but in the meantime, here are a few things to think about as you scout for viable container space.

⧉ Containers 101 ⧉

🍅 You need to use a *large* pot, 15 by 15 inches at a minimum. Bigger *is* better. Tomato plants will not grow well in a six-inch terra cotta pot, people! (Can you tell I've diagnosed that malady way too often?)

🍅 Only *one* plant per pot. Yes, it will look silly at first, but not for long.

🍅 Look for pots made of a material that won't heat up in high summer temperatures. Pulp pots, wine barrels, redwood boxes, and similar containers are great choices.

🍅 Make smart choices as to varieties. We'll talk about that in the next chapter.

🍅 Mix a nutrient-rich growing medium for your containers.

Drainage versus Water Retention

It can be confusing to hear that soil needs to retain moisture but drain effectively as well. The key to understanding this concept? Tomato roots need both water and oxygen to thrive and support growth.

On the extremes, sandy soil retains very little moisture, as water runs right through it. There's a lot of oxygen in the spaces between sand particles. Roots dry out very quickly, and you'll have to water a *lot* more often to make the plant happy.

Clay soils, on the other hand, trap moisture in the gaps between smaller clay particles, leaving very little room for oxygen. Thus the roots are hampered by living in a very moist—or wet—environment. If you're watering too much in clay soils, your plant is trying to thrive in a swamp! That's not what it wants. Imbalance, in either direction, isn't ideal for plant health and vigor.

The solution to either problem is to *aggressively and continually* incorporate organic materials. Yes, I'm repeating myself. Amend the soil! Compost, premium planting mix, leaf mold, and similar products, when mixed well with existing soils, will fill spaces in sandy soils and soak up (retain) moisture. In clay soils, the new amendments will separate clay particles, allowing water to drain through more readily. Balance is the key.

In either case, you've created a soil mix that, hopefully, performs like a sponge. Some excess water drains down below the existing root zone (and encourages roots to follow), and some water is retained in the current root zone so the plant can readily access it as needed. Voilà, happy tomato plant.

Premium potting mixes that you will use in containers, (yes, the ones that cost more) do this for you and are formulated with a balance of particles that will allow for moisture retention and drainage. Adding some compost, worm castings, and even a bit of your good garden soil to containers will add nutritive value to this mix. But don't overdo it, or you'll mess up the balance needed for sharp drainage.

❖ Gardener Alert! ❖

Before you decide to plant in containers, know this: Your container tomatoes can require more of you, the gardener, than plants in the ground. This is a growing situation that needs to be managed more closely. For those of you who completely automate your watering system and such, you're off the hook to some degree. But not entirely.

❖ Raised Up, But Not Too High ❖

Raised beds are sort of a garden/container hybrid, and can be employed almost anywhere when you decide to start, move, or enlarge your garden. Most beds equate to a really big pot. The extra volume helps roots stay cooler and provides a lot of room for growth. It also offers sharp drainage while retaining some moisture—a good thing.

Keep in mind that raised beds will usually drain faster than your native soil, especially if you've been aggressive and built thirty-inch-tall boxes. That also means you will need to water more frequently than in the non-raised beds, as with any pot, which we'll get to in the sidebar. If your beds are open at the bottom (with a hardware cloth or wire screen to keep burrowing critters out), the roots should eventually get into the native soil, so all's good. If your thirty-inch boxes are parked on the driveway next to your four-wheel hybrid, no worries there, they will be just fine.

If you're thinking that the whole raised-bed situation seems too formal, way too expensive, or too time-consuming to handle right now, know that you can make a raised bed very easily. We'll get to that, too.

⸙ Partly Cloudy, with a Chance of Tomatoes ⸙

While you examine your site, soil, and container options, there is one more reality to consider before we move ahead, especially if you're growing tomatoes for the first time: Where exactly do you live on this Google map of ours? Juneau or Johannesburg? The U.S. Gulf Coast or South America? Sydney? London? Maybe you live in a landlocked area known for its searing heat or in a hazy coastal climate.

The good news is that tomatoes grow well all over the world: hot places, cooler places, wet places, and dry places. But the climate you live in has everything to do with when your season *starts* (and ends) and thus, what *varieties* might be great choices for you. The seasonal weather patterns that your plants experience through the growing season also become a critical part of how successful your harvest will be. I trust you farmers out there are nodding in agreement.

Here's a tomato gardener's dream: a wonderfully consistent, hot but not *too* hot summer, with nice early-morning breezes and gentle soaking rains (at perfectly timed intervals) to guide your tomato plants through to a perfect harvest. Yeah, *that'll* happen!

Here are some curveballs the weather may throw at you during the season:

HIGH HEAT

Challenge: to outsmart consistent high heat or unpredictable heat waves that can prevent pollination and a good harvest. Pollination chances are greatly reduced as temperatures climb up over ninety degrees. The plant (pollen) can actually become infertile.

For starters, plant in shifts. If you plant a few seedlings each week for three to six weeks, flowers will appear in succession, and hopefully most flowers will dodge high-heat cycles. Succession-planting techniques work. While six weeks of planting isn't practical in short season zones, in many warmer climates, planting a new crop in mid-summer can extend the harvest through the fall.

[Sunscald can ruin the fruit. Don't toss that
broken patio umbrella until the season ends.]

Plant in rows that run north-south, instead of east-west. Each side of the plant gets a half day of exposure, which helps prevent the sunscald (blistering) that happens when growing fruit is in direct sunlight all day, from sunrise to sunset.

Keep a tarp, old patio umbrella, or a similar covering handy for when things really get unbearable. Use them as needed during the hottest days, usually from 10:00 A.M. to 3:00 P.M.! (And buy a big hat for yourself while you're at it.) In desert areas, where searing heat is constant, you may need to use a percentage shade cloth to cool your plants during midday heat.

HIGH HUMIDITY

When humidity arrives with summer temperatures, as it does in so many growing zones, your tomatoes will face unique challenges. Fungal diseases thrive in this condition, and since lack of moisture is not your problem, you need to manage that additional water effectively.

🍅 Grow hybrids that you know to be resistant to such afflictions.

🍅 Use soaker hoses or drip systems so you're not wetting leaves when you irrigate.

🍅 Don't water in the evening because you don't want the sun to set on a wet garden.

🍅 Plant your seedlings farther apart than you would normally, and spread your plants out on a fence or grid (rather than keeping them tightly constrained in a cage) to provide extra air circulation.

🍅 And lastly, water only as needed. Be mindful of rainfall patterns, and rainfall to date, in any given year.

How Micro Is Your Climate? I just told you that you have to listen

to your weatherman. Now I'm going to tell you to hear that, but trust yourself—your personal experience—when it comes to growing in your particular
garden.

I live in the Upper Valley of Ojai, California, at 1,500 feet. We're seventy or
so miles outside of Los Angeles, and our last possible frost date is somewhere
in late April. (Five to six weeks later than Los Angeles, most of which, in reality, can't claim a frost date at all.) Yes, like most eager 'maniacs, I don't generally honor that date with my plantings. And yes, I've been burned by late frosts
that wiped out an entire crop.

When I watch L.A. weather
reports, I generally add ten degrees
in the summer, and subtract ten
degrees in the winter. That's what
experience tells me is accurate.

In my microclimate, I also
know that the temperature during
any given day on the fringes of
the growing season can range
widely (a full forty degrees). In
canyons around us, on the floor
of the valley, or up the sides of
nearby mountains, tomato plants might
face a whole different reality. Perhaps the microclimates are
not so obvious where you live, but we've each got unique garden situations and
weather to think about so be aware of all that as you plant and grow. And hey,
for me, and many other good gardeners, blaming the "awful weather this summer" is a handy go-to excuse for a season that wasn't exactly on target.

[Our garden in Ojai.]

COLD WINTERS . . . THAT LINGER INTO SPRING

It's no fun waiting forever to plant in the spring and worrying on the other side of summer that Jack Frost might appear before the jack-o'-lantern. Use cold frames, or solid row covers, to get your plants started early. (Succession planting on the front end of the season.) And lucky you, if you have a greenhouse! If you don't, think creatively: maybe a laundry line supporting plastic sheeting? It works, and two weeks of extra growing time can mean the difference between a dismal season and a memorable one.

⁝ Tennessee Loves a Good Volunteer ⁝

(Yes, this is for you, GM.) One last thing. While you're diligently cleaning out last year's garden spot, or making room for this year's new seedlings in an entirely new space, look closely between the weeds.

"Volunteers" are those tomato seedlings that pop up seemingly out of nowhere from last year's lingering tomato energy, or a "gift" from a generous bird. Welcome those plants into this year's garden, and move them only if you must. I like to think they're good luck, even when I have no clue what variety they are. The fruit they produce will be a surprise, but it may turn out to be the most delicious find in your garden.

[
A volunteer jockeying for
position among the winter kale.
]

[Sprite, growing in our Ojai test field.]

Stripes, *Lobes,* Curves & Trusses

So many tomatoes, what's the perfect
strategy for you and your garden?

At Tomatomania events, I've heard it *all*. "My plants never seem to produce enough fruit." "I can never find that 'real tomato taste' that I remember from my childhood." "I want a *Jersey* tomato!"

I feel your pain. But maybe you just haven't chosen the *right* tomato. The good news: There are thousands of others to audition. All that diversity means you have incredible tomato opportunities ahead. Take a deep breath. You now know where you're growing so you're on your way.

The next step toward a wildly successful season? Devise a strategy. Yes, there absolutely is such a thing as a tomato-growing strategy. It can begin with one simple question: What do you want to eat?

So, will you be happiest grabbing handfuls of cherries to snack on as the season goes along, or do you want to harvest and bury your face in the hugest of huge beefsteaks in August? After all, a backyard teeming with tomatoes that you won't eat does not make for a successful season. And by the way, a resounding, *"Both!"* in answer to that question is quite acceptable! (The *huge* option also works out well if winning the largest tomato contest at the county fair is on your list of summer goals.)

The only good growing strategy is the one that works for you. Maybe you want to can, or "put up" as so many Southern grandmothers like to say, some of your crop so you can extend the season via your pantry. You *can* get exactly what you want!

❧ Saved by the . . . Gardeners? ❧

It wasn't all that many years ago tomatoes were red. Period. (Or almost red.) At least that's what most of us regular, shop-at-the-nursery-on-the-corner gardeners thought. Round, red, and medium-to-large, most were classic hybrid varieties that proved to be dependable and often disease resistant as well. Our experience in the summer was delicious, no doubt, but also pretty one-dimensional.

Meanwhile, in gardens around the globe and just down the road, the first Tomatomaniacs were growing a virtual rainbow of wonderful varieties. Savvy gardeners and farmers saved seed when, for instance, a natural mutation (a sport) occurred and a yellow pearlike tomato appeared on a plant that was supposed to produce round red tomatoes. Maybe a seed saved from a previous season (a natural cross) produced a surprise the next spring. Or maybe they were the lucky few who grew "antique" seeds that they, or their family, planted season after season. By saving the seeds from their favorite tomatoes, they preserved a rich and diverse genetic history.

While the seed-saving process might have started in Grandma's backyard, seed was inevitably shared with other tomato lovers. Farmers and good gardeners moved around, immigrated to new countries or just new parts of the country, and shared. Presto! Heirlooms of every size and shape became more and more available around the world.

Thank You, Columbus As you enjoy your heirloom tomato salad this summer, you can thank Columbus and his like-minded pals for helping spread tomatoes around the globe. That small yellow currant-style tomato first found in Peru quickly morphed into many different varieties and dishes: salsa in Mexico, sauce in Italy, and a treasure of every kind for gardeners, growers, and farmers worldwide.

The result: thousands and thousands of tomato varieties—some say more than 25,000—were brought to light and are on record today. And, in theory at least, are available somewhere in this great tomato universe of ours. Large, voluptuous, ribbed beefsteaks that often look like tiny pumpkins, gorgeous striped beauties of every shape and size, sweet bicolored gems, sugary cherries, and the widest possible spectrum of taste profiles imaginable. Something for everyone. Recent studies by plant geneticists show that tomatoes have more genes than humans—31,760, as a matter of fact.

[Great shapes and great color. Just two of the many reasons we love heirlooms.]

In more recent times, good folks and businesses began to celebrate these diverse varieties. Seed purveyors such as Renee Shepherd, expert and author Dr. Carolyn Male, savvy retailers like Gary Jones, growers like Steve Goto, organizations such as Seed Savers, and companies like Baker Creek Heirloom Seed Company began to share these garden opportunities with all of us. Then that *tiny* little thing known as the Internet exploded onto the scene. And we immediately got a better picture of the rest of the tomato world.

⌇ What Makes a Tomato an Heirloom? ⌇

At the end of the day, what's the difference between an heirloom and a hybrid? It's one of the most often asked questions at Tomatomania seedling sales and classes.

Heirloom tomatoes are most often the delicious result of the selection process that we just talked about. Gardeners motivated to re-create their success year after year saved seeds from the best tomatoes they harvested each season. I imagine that generally meant the most delicious tomatoes of the season, but they might have also saved seeds from the earliest, largest, most colorful, or most unique tomatoes in that season's harvest. After several generations (in tomato evolution, normally considered to be seven to nine) of selecting and saving for the same desired traits, a variety is generally considered "stable," meaning it should produce only the desired fruit in future generations. Voilà! You have heirloom, or "open-pollinated," seed.

All heirlooms are open-pollinated, but not all open-pollinated varieties are necessarily considered heirlooms. Some Tomatomaniacs claim that to qualify as an heirloom, a tomato must have been introduced before 1940. Experts and enthusiasts have placed heirlooms into various classes according to how they were discovered or how they were introduced to the market. If you are a true 'maniac, go back and reread (I know you read it already!) Dr. Carolyn Male's *100 Tomatoes for the American Garden* and Amy Goldman's *The Heirloom Tomato: From Garden to Table*. Great bedside table reading and full of the details you're hungry for.

The Green Zebra Effect Look at the case of Green Zebra, which was hybridized by Tom Wagner in 1983. Green Zebras are open-pollinated, so the variety qualifies as an heirloom by the base standard (and in most trade use). But, given the post–1940 creation date, it is considered a "new" or "created" heirloom and often labeled simply OP (open-pollinated), not heirloom. To the enthusiast, this offers some clarity but it can be a bit confusing to the new-comer. But in the end, no matter what it's called, it is a worthy and exciting tomato.

[Green Zebra]

❧ The Hybrid in the Room ❧

Now it's true that some heirloom fans, whether practiced gardeners or new admirers, think of hybrid tomatoes as a secondary or less rewarding garden option. Perhaps this is due to the "cardboard-tasting tomato in the grocery store in January" correlation.

That's a shame. They may not always have the catchy names or brilliant coloration of their heirloom cousins, but hybrids are terrific tomatoes with many desirable traits. They are well documented to be dependable, strong, and productive plants. If grown with good practice and picked at the peak of ripeness, they will make you one *happy* farmer.

So, what's the difference? A hybrid tomato is bred or crossed deliberately, as in racehorses and show dogs, in order to improve on or (hopefully) combine the best traits of *two* parent plants. If you save seeds from a hybrid plant and replant those seeds the next season, however, the fruit of the new plant will generally revert back to one of the parent plants or an ancestor up to two generations back. It's not yet stable. But just so we're clear, hybrid doesn't mean genetically modified (GMO)—that's an entirely different process.

Some of the world's favorite varieties are hybrids. If you've grown Better Boy and Sun Gold, Sweet 100, Early Girl, or Champion, you know what I mean. Some are classic and some are just plain nostalgic. Every gardener, especially those who have suffered disease problems in recent seasons, might benefit from including hybrid workhorses in their garden, as many have disease resistance in their pedigree.

Earning His Stripes

Brad Gates, a Northern California hybridizer, has electrified the tomato world in the last few years by introducing some of the most unique tomatoes anyone has seen to date. Michael Pollan, Haley's Purple Comet, Blue Beauty, and Sweet Carneros Pink are only a few of the striking tomatoes that gardeners everywhere are now clamoring for.

Brad is also one of the U.S. hybridizers using and developing the "blue gene" first isolated at Oregon State University. Deep blue-purple coloration carries with it the anthocyanins that makes blueberries such a healthy snack. Last time he and I chatted, Brad explained his motivation. "I started this whole enterprise because I love tomatoes, but now I do it for more than that. The people I've met along the way and the enthusiasm for growing motivates me to provide more and more interesting varieties for the home gardener each year. You'd think we'd be satisfied with the thousands of tomato varieties available on the market today, yet we strive for better, more exciting, more bizarre varieties to enjoy. We can't wait to see what we find in the garden next season!" I can't wait either and know that Brad will continue to amaze and inspire us to grow new and unique varieties every spring.

[Brad Gate's Sweet Carneros Pink.]

[Wild Boar Farms' Blue Beauty.]

[Mary Robinson's German Bi-color (yellow) and Red Pear Pinform (red).]

❖ Tomato Classes ❖

Let's dive right in. Here's what's out there for your growing and eating pleasure:

BEEFSTEAKS

A slice of one of these large beauties will smother that hamburger patty and amaze your neighbors and friends—and let's be honest, you know the latter is one of your goals for the season! They'll grow to one pound or larger, are often flattened to some degree, and many are wonderfully ribbed like a pumpkin. (The world-record beefsteak, a hybrid called Delicious, weighed in at a whopping seven pounds, twelve ounces!) These are the tomatoes you remember from your childhood. They have the taste that, for many, defines summer.

Most beefsteaks are late-summer producers, so you'll need to be an attentive and *patient* farmer. They can also be very large, heavy plants. And while most will produce enthusiastically, they will never match the production rates of smaller tomato varieties, and some can be a bit stingy. But I get it. Every bite is *so* worth it.

A few favorites: Kellogg's Breakfast, Dr. Wyche's Yellow, Brandywines of every color and strain, Beefsteak (yes, that's a named variety as well), Gold Medal, Cherokee Purple, German Pink, Ananas Noire, Big Zac, Black Krim, Zapotec, Missouri Pink Love Apple, and the aforementioned Delicious are all rightfully popular varieties in the beefsteak category.

SLICERS (GLOBES)

Slicers are the perfect round, medium-large tomato, just right for your BLT. Slicers and globes can be found in every color of the rainbow, and now in a variety of stripes as well. You might find slicers in attractive clusters at the grocery store. Imagine growing those in your backyard!

A few favorites: Earl of Edgecombe, Sweet Tangerine, Lemon Boy, Woodle Orange, Better Boy, Carmello, Black, Thessaloniki, and Momotaro.

OXHEARTS

These tomatoes are a most underappreciated lot, maybe because oxhearts are so fantastically strange looking. They are sort of oblong, often heart-shaped or even blocky, and you'll never find two fruits on the same plant that look alike—all part of their charm. Generally thought of as a cooking or paste tomato, oxhearts are typically meaty and dense with few seeds. On top of all that, they're delicious eaten fresh.

The plant's wispy or weepy appearance (part of its gene pool and more pronounced in some varieties than in others) puts some gardeners off and may hinder your growing season in super-hot areas because that leaf and branching style provides far less shade cover than thick sturdy foliage. I used to think that oxhearts, while better tasting, didn't produce as much as more standard paste or cooking varieties. But I've since been proven wrong on that assumption.

"Heart" or "strawberry" in the name is a sure sign you've found an oxheart variety. A few favorites: Reif Red Heart, German Orange Strawberry, Bread and Salt, Carol Chyko's Big Paste Black, Orange Russian 117, New Zealand Pink Pear, Lemon Oxheart, Amish Paste, and Brad's Black Heart are other good varieties to be on the lookout for.

SALADETTES

The four- to six-ounce fruit fits really nicely in the palm of your hand. The shiny, plum-sized saladettes slice up beautifully into four or eight pieces, so they're perfect for your salad. (Hmm, wonder where it got that name?) Chefs like them because they are so pretty and symmetrical on the inside. I always think these look like plums, but your grocery store will sell Roma-type fruits as plum tomatoes, which always confuses me. A plum tomato should look like, well, a plum, right? Some in this class will rival cherries for productivity.

A few favorites: "Hall of Famer" Green Zebra, Black Prince, Siberian, Pink Ping Pong, Stupice, Jaune Flamme, Sweet Carneros Pink, Tolstoi, Red Boar, and Sungella are good examples of this category.

ROMA OR PASTE-TYPES

The standard bearer, the classic Italian San Marzano, now has cousins in every color and size. Roma-types or sauce/paste tomatoes are typically on the dryer side, have fewer seeds (a fact that some need to pay attention to), and are a breeze to process for canning. While not often on the top of the list for plucking-and-eating-in-the-garden deliciousness, they are great for salads and sauces. They provide color and mass, you provide a little extra dressing, spice, or seasoning. *But* some of the larger, longer, and pepper-shaped Roma types, however, are among the tastiest varieties you will ever eat.

Many are compact plants and produce really well, but Roma-types are also prone to blossom end rot, a malady that usually hits early in the season. (Health Kick is one compact red variety that's never shown blossom end rot in our summer trials.)

A blocky or elongated oval shape is the hallmark of many paste or Roma-type varieties.

Cherries, grapes, and pears are the jewels of summer, adding color and excitement to both gardens and salads.

The list of Roma-type favorites includes Striped Roman, Opalka, Viva Italia, Big Mama, Long Tom, Federle, Sweet Orange Roma, Polish Linguisa, Martino's Roma, Golden Rave, and the previously mentioned Health Kick and San Marzano. If you can't get enough of San Marzano, try the golden variety or the larger ones, San Marzano Redorta or San Marzano Gigante!

CHERRIES, GRAPES, AND PEARS

You know this one. Your taste buds will tell you that these are the sweetest of the lot (scientists agree with you), and the buckets of bright fruit you'll pick will prove they are also the most productive you can buy. Cherries are definitely round, while grape tomatoes tend to be a bit more elongated. They look like . . . grapes. (Imagine that.) And let's not forget pear tomatoes, which have that curvy va-va-voom appeal. Nothing is sexier in a salad.

These plants might be shrubby or huge and rambling, so give them some room—and some support. (Or if you're in a rebellious mood, let them fall wildly over a terrace or retaining wall.) These beauties, especially the currant varieties, are the closest genetic match to the first tiny yellow fruits found growing on a hillside in South America centuries ago.

A few favorites: Spoon, Black Cherry, Green Doctors, Gardener's Delight, Snow White, Sun Gold, Sweet 100, Sweet Treats, Orange Paruche, Michael Pollan, Sugar Snack, Red Fig, Yellow Pear, and Chocolate Cherry are just a few in this popular category.

Tomato 101 In the tomato recipe world, the divisions, or classes, of tomatoes that just made you salivate here are generally assigned different uses in the kitchen. Yes, some are easier to process (cook, can, and the like), some will be juicier or dryer, some will have few seeds and others tons of seed.

That's just how it is, but don't be afraid to break the rules when it comes to devouring your crop! Any tomato is a sauce tomato if you try hard enough. Cherry tomatoes are amazing in salsa (make a rainbow salsa—gorgeous) and yes, beefsteaks make a great sauce. Carry on.

❧ Pick Me! Pick Me! ❧

People often ask which tomato variety is my favorite. Easy. The last one I ate.

Yes, I'm always after great taste. I really do enjoy the wide spectrum of tomato flavors that come with all the unique varieties, colors, and even different sizes of tomatoes. I want all of that every season, so my growing strategy is simple: I want *a lot* of tomatoes.

To that end, I will usually grow more small-to-medium-size varieties than huge beefsteaks, simply because they tend to be more productive. But if you snuck into my garden last year, you could easily see that I grew *a lot* of *everything*. Affirmative.

[Big Momma, Patty's Yellow-Striped Beefsteak, and Golden San Marzano prove that tomatoes can be as pretty on the inside as out.]

⚜ Scott's Hall of Famers ⚜

A single favorite? Impossible. But here are twelve standouts—at least until next season.

A. **Missouri Pink Love Apple.** Could you pass that up at a sale? A bright pink, round, and utterly delicious beefsteak.

B. **Cherokee Purple.** Classic for a good reason. For me and for many of you, no doubt, it sets the pace for heirloom taste.

C. **Orange Paruche.** A relatively new find for me, and yes, I still think this sweet orange cherry outshines Sun Gold. Just sayin'.

D. **Spoon.** A super-tiny, red currant-type that packs a major flavor punch, even if it *is* a bit difficult to pick!

E. **Michael Pollan.** A sexier-looking Green Zebra (it's a selection of this classic) with all the same tang. And who doesn't want to have Michael Pollan over for dinner?

F. **Haley's Purple Comet.** Beautiful, unique, and tasty—all I need.

G. **Sweet Tangerine.** I once picked more than twenty-five gorgeous orange and blemish-free fruits off a medium-size plant, and still had weeks and weeks of tasty tomatoes to come. Enough said.

H. **Carol Chyko's Big Paste Black.** The most unique fruit you'll ever harvest. Enormous, misshapen, and mouth-watering.

I. **Black and Brown Boar.** All the fantastic taste of a black tomato in a gorgeous striped package.

J. **Gold Medal.** You'll swoon at how beautiful the great big fruit is, and then the sweet and citrusy flavors of this bicolor beauty will take you to new heights.

K. **Yellow Brandywine.** While it is hard to ignore any member of the Brandywine clan, this is my favorite of the bunch.

L. **Jaune Flamme.** Uniquely tangy and an early producer, a gorgeous orange saladette.

Now I feel badly because I left out about fifty other favorites!

Santiam

Open Pollinated

EARLY and tasty. Makes sense to most gardeners! Small red short-season choice that produces nicely on a tidy plant. Great for containers.

65 Days   DET

TOMATOMANIA!

Your followers
will be all
a **twitter**
if you share
a pic of me!

Santiam

Let's Go *Shopping*

Tomato lingo and deciphering a tomato label

You've done some great homework up to this point. Your garden business plan is in place, you're developing a strategy, and spring is imminent. Let the shopping begin!

We shop everywhere these days. You may be buying seedlings online, through catalogs, at the nursery around the corner, or at one of our Tomatomania events. Wherever you're making your choices, you have more information to consider before you bring your new babies home. Oh, and bring a big truck! (Not to worry, a Fiat works just fine, too.)

Tomatoes and the wine country are a perfect match. A sale at Cornerstone Sonoma.

As the early birds gather at the gate at our inaugural Maryland sale.

The Roots of Tomatomania

So how did this whole mania thing get started? Well, it's no secret that tomatoes have long been the (love) apple of many a gardener's eye. And for a good number of us, tomato seedlings are an exciting and very literal sign of spring.

Gary Jones, the owner of Pasadena's much-touted, and much-missed, Hortus, really got tomato lovers excited with the launch of the first Tomatomania event back in 1994. He worked with forward-thinking organic farmers Barbara and Bill Spencer of Windrose Farm (Paso Robles, California) and Pasadena-area tomato grower Steve Goto to provide a unique selection of rare heirloom seedlings that customers had never seen, let alone grown, before. The event was a hit (a phenomenon!) from the beginning. A one-day lineup of twenty-five varieties soon gave way to a four-day extravaganza with more than 275 different tomato offerings. *Crazy!*

I joined the nursery team in 1995, after many years of trying to convince myself that a corporate marketing career was the right path for me. I will be forever grateful that Gary gave me the nod and welcomed me aboard. It was a major (tomato) turning point in my life.

As the event picked up steam, Tomatomania became the nursery's busiest weekend of the year. We hosted a wonderful garden gumbo of CEOs and soccer moms, grandmothers and urban hipsters, hard-core gardeners and eager first-timers at the event each season. Maybe you were there? It was an incredibly exciting time. Nothing made me happier then, as now, than a crazy long weekend of tomato talk.

Unfortunately, after ten or so meteoric years, the nursery was suddenly forced to close in 2000. Garden glitterati from San Diego to Santa Barbara were devastated. I made it my goal to keep this one important piece of the nursery very much alive. That spring, Gary and I, along with friend and former Hortus staffer Kate Karam, produced the first weekend Tomatomania event outside the nursery. The faithful showed up in droves. Long story short, I eventually took over the reins, and, with the blessings of my former partners and the support of a loyal and enthusiastic team, Tomatomania has grown into a larger series of multiday events that we've produced in twenty cities and on both the east and west coasts. Sometimes it's hard to believe we are now the largest tomato seedling sale in the nation. *Really crazy.*

❧ Decoding a Tomato Label or Description ❧

Here's hoping the suppliers and growers you support will provide a helpful staff and *way* more varietal information than you will ever need. But sometimes it doesn't quite work out that way, which is why it pays to know your way around a tomato label or description.

You may find codes and letters that are confusing at first, but have no fear. These are all good things, even crucial things, to know, and easy to understand once you know the meaning of all that tomato talk.

﹖ John Hancock ﹖

Find an intriguing photograph of a tomato, or one with a sexy name? Take a closer look. The names of some of these tomatoes are not only fun, but can also give you clues about their heritage, notable qualities, or their performance in the garden. And the pictures will just make your mouth water.

﹖ Name, Rank, and Serial Number ﹖

The varietal description on the label will tell you more about the fruit's size, plant size, color, and maybe even a few quirky facts about the plant you are considering. The tag should definitely tell you whether it is an heirloom or a hybrid. Notes on taste, while subjective, of course, might also be featured there to tempt you. Certain descriptions are almost impossible to resist ("tastes like sunshine"), I know, but weigh all the available information carefully against your unique growing situation and seasonal strategy.

Label-ese. In catalog-speak, some hybrids are called exactly that on the label, such as a Sun Gold Hybrid. Others, like Better Boy, may not have the word "hybrid" in the name, depending on where you are considering making your purchases (catalog, Web site, seedling sale?).

Over the years, I've learned that tomato folks tend to do as they please (we're funny that way), but in general, many sources go by the mantra that unless a seed or seedling is specifically labeled "heirloom," it is indeed a hybrid. Now you know.

⁖ Determinate or Indeterminate? ⁖

Look for a *D* or *I* on the label, or sometimes, DET or IND. This will tell you the growth habit of the plant you are considering.

In general, determinates tend to be smaller and more compact plants than their counterparts. They bloom on the terminal (main) stem, and when that happens, upward growth ceases. Determinate plants also tend to produce fruit in larger sets (more fruit at one time) and with many, the fruit "holds well" (stays put) on the vine until you are ready to harvest a basketful, if all goes well throughout the season.

Indeterminate plants will cover the patio, grow up to the gutters, and maybe even engulf their neighbor plants if not contained (or hide your actual neighbors, which might be a good thing). Some varieties can be *huge*. This is not a bad thing, just an example of how plants grow differently. The indeterminate plant does not fruit at the top of the main stem, so it keeps growing and producing fruit along the main stem and on side branching.

Which is better? Well, that depends. What's your strategy?

⁖ Your Days Are Numbered ⁖

Look more closely at the description and you will see Days to Maturity, Number of Days, or DTM listed somewhere. It's all about when you likely will be *picking* that first fruit.

This is a major plot point in your tomato movie: DTM is the approximate number of days between planting that six-week-old seedling and picking your first piece of fruit. The key word here is *approximate*. This number assumes perfect conditions and growing practice, so you will see some major flexing there.

Truly, all that number really tells you is whether you are growing an early, mid-season, or late-season tomato variety. If a tag says ninety days, in most cases, you will be picking *after* 110 days. I know, right? Who comes up with the logic on these things?

As far as I'm concerned, "under seventy days" is generally considered early, "seventy to ninety days" mid-season, and beyond that, you're in late-season territory—and picking at the end of the summer. Use this knowledge as part of your strategy.

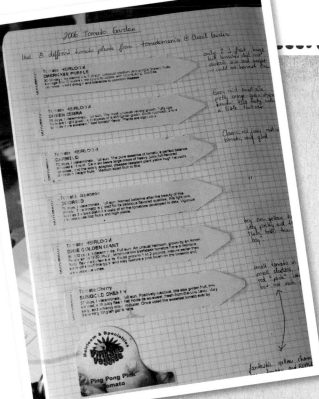

[I wish I were this organized]

MDLC (The Mysterious Disappearing Label Conundrum)

And while we're talking about labels, know this: They seem to grow legs and run away during the season. They really do. How does that happen? Who knows? And if they don't disappear, they always seem to bleach out in the hot summer sun, so you can't read the label anyway. So whether you're growing six varieties or a field full of plants, this could be a problem. Trust me. You won't remember what's what as the season goes along.

Some maniacs will attach the tag to the top of the stake or cage, photocopy labels, make elaborate journals, or otherwise devise clever solutions to this problem. I generally make a rough sketch or chart of the garden once all of my plants are in place—my version of name recognition software. (And p.s., make two copies, and put at least one in an obvious place so you won't lose it.)

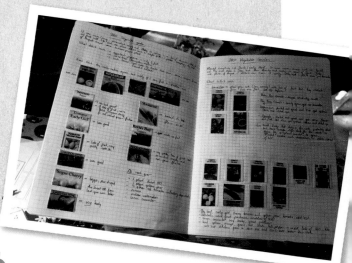

Got Your Tomato Ph.D.?

As you shop for seedlings, you may notice that hybrid variety names are often followed by capital letters, as one might apply to doctors and others with advanced degrees. In the tomato world, this signifies that the hybridizer of that variety considers it resistant to a certain disease or malady.

That resistance could be based on its parentage, field tests, or both. The capital letter *N*, for instance, implies resistance to Nematodes. *V* refers to verticillium wilt, *F* to fusarium wilt, and so forth. I'm afraid that no, you won't find an *H* for hornworms. Nothing so far is resistant to those buggers!

Greenhouse Dreams? If you're into tomato discovery and locating hard-to-find varieties like we are at Tomatomania, perhaps you're also the brave soul who seeks out and starts his or her own seeds. I salute you! I did that. Once.

Thing is, I'm just way too busy in the early spring to give seeds and tiny new seedlings the attention they need. These days, and for my events, I'm happy to let dedicated growers start seed (and they do it exceedingly well). But if you have the time, and a good seed starting setup, it can be a lot of fun. You will need to scan online seed and varietal descriptions for the same critical information we've discussed here. Just be sure to come to Tomatomania when you need to find a few more really unique varieties you didn't grow in seedling trays!

[Now, if you have a greehouse this size . . .]

[Potatoe Leaf Variety]

❧ Finding the One ❧

Do you want the large plant with the flowers on it, or the little stocky guy over there in the corner? First and foremost, *choose a sturdy, green seedling.* That's the bottom line.

Check for spotting on the leaves and inspect the plant closely. Be on the lookout for any random aphids and their friends. You don't want to bring them home to your garden. If there is a good selection of the variety you want, choose the plant *without* flowers. I'm going to suggest you remove those anyway when we get to the planting stage.

You may be surprised at the variation in leaf shape and color between varieties on the sales shelf. In addition to the standard tomato leaf you're used to seeing, you may find sturdy-looking, potato-leafed varieties (which some believe to be more resistant to leaf diseases than others), or some that appear more wispy, or even weepy. (Remember those oxhearts?) In my garden book, none is truly better or worse, only different. Try them all!

[Standard or regular tomato leaf]

61

You Won't Find This on Any Label Okay, so here's what one 'maniac named Kyle asked on our Tomatomania Facebook page recently: "I want a tomato I can eat while I drive. Any suggestions?"

I have to admit, I've been asked a lot of "which variety" questions, but I'd personally never considered choosing a tomato based on that criteria. Any bite-sized cherry tomato is a good candidate for its snack-friendly size, no knife required, but an everyday cherry doesn't quite have that pizzazz you need to get through a traffic jam. I recommended Blush, a sweeter than sweet, super-elongated cherry variety that happens to be yellow with red splashes, like a stoplight. Drive carefully out there, Kyle.

❧ Remember, It's All About You ❧

Some of you will choose larger plants, some smaller. Make yourself *happy*.

Spoiler alert: If you follow the guidelines in the next chapter, they will all look the same size when you get them into the garden!

[Tomatomania creates a planting frenzy at White Fower Farm.]

Plant Me *Already!*

Plant, water, and feed your seedlings
correctly to get a solid start

Ready? I know you are. I sure am. Let's get out there and do this thing.

When you decided where you would plant this year, maybe you had plenty of time to add soils and other rich organic materials to that space. Whether your soil has been prepped or not, it's time to add even more of all that to make a rich new home for your seedlings——they will be so appreciative of your efforts.

Now, we're going to take a look at the simple steps that will make your soil and your new tomato seedling very happy:

AMEND *liberally*.

DIG *deep*.

PLANT *deep*.

FERTILIZE *wisely*.

READY? Let's get on with it!

⁚ Soils "R" Us ⁚

If the soil in your chosen garden spot turns over easily with a shovel and you can add even more compost and planting mix, do it. It's just not advisable to slam a new seedling into the questionable, and perhaps clay-filled, native soils in many of our gardens. If the soil is raw and tough, turn what you can, and then layer amendments on top. Be liberal. You've already got your bagged materials, maybe compost from your garden, animal manures, or green manure (hay, straw) ready to add richness to the soil. Pile it on. Go right ahead. Tomatoes will grow but will not fruit well on a low-calorie diet.

Breaking News: The New Soil Strategy That Saves Time (and Your Back)

I know it sounds like a gossip magazine's empty promise, but modern plant science really does tell us that it is not necessary, and truly not advisable, to aggressively turn the soil in your entire garden over in preparation for planting each year or season.

Why? Soil health is all about microorganisms, which set up systems and live in particular strata within the soil. Mixing and turning the soil kills, discourages, or displaces those organisms and interrupts what may be a super system that will readily support your new plants. Layering rich organic amendments on top of the soil, season after season, gets the job done. Some call that the "lasagna method," I call it the "forest method." Forests have been doing this successfully for millions of years.

But if you're in a new space, and want to know more about the soil base while easing the entry for new seedlings, please make an exception in year one so that you have the opportunity to learn more about your new environment. Go for it. Dig up, plow, or otherwise break into the ground space. (Or hire someone *else* to do it!) And pay close attention to what you find there.

The ages'-old practice of double digging has been encouraged for years, and while it will disturb the soil systems as just highlighted, it is a fantastic way to mix good, new, organic matter deep into the soil. But after you double dig that first year, believe me, you—and your back—will be happy for new soil science in the years to come. Bring on the lasagna—extra thick.

Run for Cover

We all want to plant as early as possible in the spring season. It's only natural. Who can wait? If you do want to plant early, here's the key: Provide cover (be creative!), and hence warmth, for your new seedlings (see Cold Winters That Linger into Spring, page 24). Heat is key to strong early growth. You'll be way ahead of the game when temperatures rise to meet you.

Dig Deep, Plant Deep

Dig deep. Regardless of how much you dug around in the garden in preparation for the season, you need to dig a deep hole in the spot where you will actually plant your new seedling. A *deep* hole. This will loosen the soil and encourage fast root growth. I have friends who get out the post-hole digger to accomplish this task, and frankly, that's a really good idea.

How deep do you dig? How much patience and energy have you got? In most gardens, if you can go down twelve to fifteen inches, you're golden. Do what you can. If you can't get there, that's okay.

Plant deep. Take a seedling out of its pot, loosen the root ball slightly, and remove any flowers visible on the plant. Wait, what?! You just dug a fifteen-inch hole for a six-inch seedling? Congratulations!

Fill the bottom of that beautiful hole with your wonderfully amended soil, and set the seedling in the hole so that only three inches of the plant will be visible above the soil after planting.

Remove any leaves that will get buried under the soil line, and add more amended soil and a bit more fertilizer around the root ball. Press the seedling firmly into its new home, leaving a slight depression around the base of the plant that will catch water when you irrigate. (A small circular berm to contain water is a bonus.) You've just created the ideal space for this plant to grow.

Yes, you'll bury some (or often plenty) of the stem. That's the idea. Roots will quickly develop all along the buried section. In very short order, the plant will be sturdier and happier. The increased capacity to absorb water and food will support steady and strong plant growth. Bottom line, it's a good start. If you are planting a bit late and temperatures are

[Yes, a deep hole.]

What does Organic Really Mean? At its most basic, organic materials are those that were once alive. These natural materials break down into nutrients that plants can easily access. Organic amendments, fertilizers, and growing techniques are natural, effective, and, most important, not chemicals.

[Fed, watered, and mulched. One happy plant.]

already on the rise, you've also now made a deep and cool home for the new root ball. That's what the plant wants. Good going.

Now, add a bit more fertilizer at the base of the plant. Water around the root zone well. Repeat. Do it once more for good measure. You've completely soaked the root ball. That's the goal for the whole season. Soak the root ball when you water. (I'll give you more water guidelines in the next chapter.) You shouldn't have to water again for three, four, or even five days. A two-inch layer of mulch added around the base of the plant will help retain this moisture. Move on to the next seedling.

⁏ Graft Is the Word ⁏

One of the trends taking hold in our horticultural community is the use of plant grafting techniques with tomatoes. (Incidentally, we're late to this party, as it's been done in other parts of the world for years.) As with stone fruits, citrus, and even roses, tomato plants are now being grafted to add strength, vigor, and disease resistance to small seedlings.

How it works: The tomato variety you buy is grafted onto a sturdy root stock (a completely separate plant that is the "gatekeeper") that will hopefully provide some resistance to soil-related and vascular diseases that can get to the plant through the roots. If you plant grafted seedlings and bury the plant deep, you've defeated the point. Roots will grow from *both* sections of the plant and resistance to disease may be lost. Plant the seedling out in the garden *at the same level as it is in its smaller pot*.

Meanwhile, in New England . . .

Gardeners in cold winter areas, listen up: If you are pushing the boundaries of your last frost date when you plant (something I wholeheartedly support if you're willing to coddle your plants for a bit), your soils are still cool. Maybe even cold, too cold to encourage rapid root and plant growth, if you've truly dug a deep hole.

In order to avoid cooler temperatures farther down in the soil, dig a shallow trench rather than a deep hole to make the most of the stem-rooting advantage. Lay the plant on its side in the trench, covering all but three inches of the tip. Yes, it'll look a little funny lying at an angle, but in short order the plant will straighten up and you're on your way. (Keep some plastic handy in case things cool off too much!)

The Twenty-Minute Raised Bed I promised you a hint or two on the easiest way to make a raised bed, so here you go: Fill your wheelbarrow with a great mix of rich planting soil and compost. Dump it in the area you've decided is best for your tomatoes. Repeat. Repeat again. Keep adding this rich soil until the bed is large enough and high enough to house all the tomatoes you want to grow. How high? Ten inches, great. Fifteen, even better. Level the top slightly and compact the top gently with the back of a shovel. There you have it, a raised bed.

Pretty simple, right? No need for fancy (expensive) borders and thirty inches of soil. You're on your way.

For a little structure, use hay bales, cinder blocks, or even logs as "borders" if you like. Either way, a raised berm gives your plants all the same advantages of a fancy raised bed, without the time and expense.

[Any type of raised bed can be an advantage.]

❧ Elbow Room ❧

This is a garden, remember, not a clown car. How many seedlings can your space reasonably support? Ideally, plants should be as much as six feet apart to allow sun to hit all parts of the plant, prevent competition, and to allow perfect air circulation between plants.

I can hear you scoffing. For most of us that seems absurd, right? Beneficial, yes, but absurd. Those of you with larger properties or vegetable gardens may be able to allow for that space. But I suspect that even if you have a large space, like many 'maniacs, you try to squeeze in more plants than would be comfortable there. If ten plants can fit in thirty square feet, then just think how many plants you can fit in three hundred square feet, right?! Leave about 3 feet between each plant for best results.

Plant other like-minded plants, meaning those that thrive in similar growing conditions (basil, onions, and just about any garden herb), among the tomatoes so you can spread your garden out without wasting space.

❧ Feed Me, Seymour ❧

Tomatoes are greedy plants. They'll hungrily use all the fertilizer you give them. And if overfed, you will probably be rewarded with a huge and healthy green plant. You'll feel like a very successful gardener.

Thing is, there may not be a tomato in sight. Plants that are overfed seem to figure that they have plenty of time to bear fruit and will drop their flowers like crazy. No flowers, no fruit.

Fertilize wisely. Choose a balanced organic fertilizer to get the plants everything they will need throughout the season. Feed per the product's directions as you plant. Feed a second time as the flowers begin to appear on your plants, which is usually about five to six weeks along, give or take a week depending on your garden and varietal choices. In most gardens (those planted in the ground with at least decent soil) that's all the fertilizer the plants will need during the season. *Twice.* That's it.

Tomato Dodge Ball (Succession Planting) Tomato plants
will flower as part of the cycle that begins when you plant. They won't all flower at exactly the same time since they will fruit at different times (you know this already). But eventually, you'll see at least some flowering on most of your plants. When your plants do flower, summer temperatures can simultaneously be high in many areas. Above 90 degrees, pollen may be rendered infertile, so if your plants are flowering during a heat wave, you may get no fruit as a result. Not what you're after.

The good news: Heat waves run in cycles. If you have the time and the space, plant a few seedlings at regular intervals over the next thirty or even sixty days. If you do that, all of your plants won't flower at the same time. And who knows, you just might outsmart Mother Nature.

[Even the flowers that start the
fruiting process will look different
from variety to variety.]

[Get everything you'll need for the
season, so it's ready when you need it.]

ꞔ Exceptions to the Fertilizing Rule ꞔ

We know by now that in home farming, there are always exceptions.

🍅 Sandy soils or hilly plantings shed water, and consequently fertilizer, much more quickly.
Up the ante and feed these plants at least once a month.

🍅 Containers also shed water and fertilizer more quickly, but in a much smaller space. Feed
container plants at least every ten days.

🍅 If your plant choices include beefsteak varieties, you have a long season to manage before
you get fruit. Add a third light feeding ten to twelve weeks after planting to push the
plants through the end of the season.

Now, the hard part! Waiting for your fruit to ripen . . .

Fertilizer 1-2-3

When you purchase fertilizer, you should see three numbers displayed prominently on the packaging. The numbers, the NPK, represent the amount or percentage of nitrogen, phosphorous, and potassium in the package and the balance between them. These are the major nutrients that plants will need during the growing season and the most important thing to provide for your new tomatoes. Seek a balance in the numbers. Remember, 30-0-0 is lawn fertilizer.

Trace elements, mineral supplements, worm castings, and all other natural additives are a bonus, and I encourage you to do as much of that as you want. Some 'maniacs add fish heads, crushed egg shells, Epsom salts or aspirin to their in-ground recipe (aspirin was originally derived from salicylic acid in willows, a plant that home gardeners have used for thousands of years to encourage root growth). Go for it.

Synthetic fertilizers tend to have higher NPK numbers than organic products. In our super-sized world, we're often seduced by that idea. Organics are just as effective, and much better for your soil.

Liquid fertilizers (root soak or foliar application) such as fish emulsion, compost tea, and kelp mixes are also phenomenal extras during the season, especially for container plantings. Tread lightly, though, as some are not as balanced as others. When you apply a foliar food the plants actually absorb this nutrition through the leaves, so you will see the difference in your plants almost immediately.

Support Your Local *Tomato*

Staking, tying, and the "Do I pinch?" question

Once planted, tomatoes are generally agreeable little garden dwellers, and just know that we're not dealing with a fragile and needy plant here. Relax, it'll be tougher than most of your weeds. You've already done most of the hard work with all that garden analyzing, strategizing, shopping, and planting.

But we have more work to do. It isn't particularly difficult to water, pinch, and stake your plants effectively, but this is where it counts!

⁓ Don't Water Like a 'Maniac

Okay, so after your new seedlings were planted in the garden, you watered them well. You know the rule of thumb when you irrigate is to "soak the root ball." It doesn't take much water to do that with a new 4-inch seedling, but that's what I want you to do *each* time you water during the season.

Early in any given tomato year, temperatures are often more reasonable (okay, maybe not if you live in Phoenix), and you've just given your plant more room than it has ever had and a lot of encouragement in the form of fertilizer. While all situations are different (and remember, we're talking in-ground planting here, not pots), chances are you won't have to irrigate again for three, four, or maybe even five days. Watch the top of the soil. Still dark? Plant still looks perky? It's *fine*.

Water the seedling again when the top of the soil dries out a bit. *Soak* it again. The plant will absorb all the water it possibly can given its root size. Then, some moisture is going to sink down below the root zone, urging the roots to follow. And that's what we want. As the season progresses, the root ball will get larger and larger. And so should the amount of water you deliver to the plant when you irrigate.

❧ Thunderstorm Alley ❧

In Southern California and other Mediterranean climates, we rarely get summer rain, so it's easy for us to regulate how much water our plants get. Not so much if you live where summer thunderstorms are plentiful.

If that is your situation, there are years, I suspect, when you wish you had a retractable roof over the garden, right? Watch those rainfall amounts closely, and adjust your watering schedule accordingly. Some seasons you may not need to add *any* additional water.

❧ Water Willpower ❧

When fruit appears on the plant, it's difficult for most of us to stick to an infrequent watering schedule. But, if you've been watering deeply all season, the plant will use its reserves to get though this schedule. Most tomatoes will get their drought-tolerant merit badges during this part of the season.

As the fruit begins to ripen (and yes, this is counter-intuitive), cut back on the watering schedule even more. Seasoned veterans and many savvy farmer's market growers will cut their water off entirely at this point. Sounds harsh, but here's the rub: The amount of water you give the plants toward the end of the season has *everything* to do with how your tomatoes will taste. And great taste, it goes without saying, is every gardener's goal.

In the beginning of the season, all the water the

plant takes in supports the healthy growth of stems, leaves, and roots. But toward the end of the season, the plant's energy (and the water) is directed to the fruit. More water in the fruit dilutes flavor as it disrupts the sugar-acid balance that we have been waiting for all summer. I'm thinking that's probably *not* what you want. Again, less water, tastier fruit. Simple, right?

[Soak it!!]

The Miss America Syndrome

It's summer, temperatures are soaring. Your plants are growing well and are full of ripening fruit. But the plants look awful! They were so green and spry in the spring and now they're yellowing, there are holes in the leaves, and they're leaning way off the stakes. . . .

Give your plants a break! This is not the Miss America Pageant. We're not looking for pretty plants, we want copious amounts of delicious fruit! Yes, some plants will look better than others in late summer. But hey, they're all taking a purposeful, yet inevitable, stroll toward the compost pile. Not quite ready for this at mid-season (I'm talking about you and me here, not the plant), our tendency is to try and "fix it" by watering more as the plant tires and the fruit gets larger and larger.

Try as you might, that just won't work. The plant will look worse as the season progresses because that's how Mother Nature intended it to be. All the plant's energy is being directed to the fruit. After all, the plant's true goal is to make seeds, that circle-of-life thing. Let it happen. Don't get crazy with the hose. Your taste buds will thank you later.

Seriously, put down the hose.

[Don't be tempted.]

⁙ Containers: The Squeaky Wheel ⁙

Container growers, heads-up here. You're in a whole different ball game given sharp drainage and no moisture reserves for the roots to get to!

Your pots, no matter how large, will need more regular water than those planted in soil. Period. A lot more. In high summer, I end up watering my pots at least once a day and sometimes more if the pots are in all-day sun. (This is also another reason for placing containers in a spot where they will get the sun they need, but not super-stressful exposure all day.)

Watch your plants closely and consider your planting location. Water accordingly.

⁙ Sucker! ⁙

With your expert care, the main stem of your new seedling will stretch skyward, and you will begin to see thickening of that stem, larger and glorious-looking leaves, and some new growth (branching) along the stem. This is natural, of course, as the plant grows, a good sign. New branches appear just above the point where leaves meet the main stem. If the leaves and leaf nodes are widely spaced, this process can be orderly and easy to assess. With some varieties, it's complete chaos.

Some will call this "sucker" growth, alluding to what some grafted trees and roses often produce during a given season. But in reality, it's not the same. If eager shoots appear at the base of a rose in your garden, below the line or knot that is the graft point, you're definitely looking at vigorous sucker growth that will, in fact, sap the plant's strength. That's the root stock growing. If left to grow and flower, that branch may just dominate the rest of the rose growth above it given its vigorous nature. Most important, and inevitably, this new branching will flower, but the bloom will be a different, and most often, less desirable rose than you intended to grow. No gardener wants that. *But on a tomato, it's not truly sucker growth at all.*

Side branching will grow, flower, and fruit just like the rest of the plant. It will also make your plant thicker, shade lower growth more, and give you a bigger plant to hold up and deal with. Bottom line, all this growth makes the plant bulkier.

Yes, this does literally weigh on the plant. If all side branching is left to grow, the energy of the plant is divided among many branches rather than a few. Result? You end up with

[Pinching? New branching at the base of the leaf is your target.]

more tomatoes, but smaller or more variable-sized fruit than otherwise. If that's part of your strategy, you're right on track. (I'm betting you won't even notice this if you're growing cherries and smaller varieties.) But with beefsteaks and other large varieties, you very well may be able to see the difference. So what's a gardener to do?

❧ To Pinch or Not to Pinch? ❧

This new side branching is quite easy to pinch off by hand. But do you absolutely need to remove this growth to have a successful season? No. Will pinching make the plant more manageable? Yes. It will be smaller and less dense.

This is another strategy point. If you have a field full of plants and don't happen to have a backyard gardening crew (right?), chances are, you won't do anything. That's okay. If you are growing three indeterminate plants in large pots on a small patio, you need to at least think about some kind of sprawling plant-growth management strategy—or you may not have much patio space left for those romantic summer dinners (the mosquitoes would miss you terribly). If you're a coastal grower who needs more heat, pinch. Growing in Phoenix or other hot areas? Careful with the pinching, you need leaf cover.

Growers looking to produce *huge* tomatoes pinch like crazy. Tomatoes vying for world-record status might be the only fruit on an entire plant (seriously), since the gardener pinches not only branching, but the flowers as well. All the energy of the plant is directed to that one fruit, which is then likely to be enormous. Eureka! First prize.

Some commercial or farmers' market growers only pinch new growth on the bottom of the plant. Doing that focuses the subsequent growth upward, so they don't end up with huge, shrubby lower sections. A good idea, for farmers at least, as these growers are usually planting more densely than most of us will at home. Others pinch up to the first "fruit set," while some continue to pinch all season. Then there are growers (guilty here) who don't pinch *at all*. And we all end up with great fruit.

One caveat: If you're growing determinate plants, be careful how much you pinch, since your plant will be smaller to start. You may want some extra branching. With indeterminates, and since this is *your* garden, you can pinch as much, and as often, as you like. Most backyard gardeners will pinch at least a little as the season goes along.

And if you don't pinch . . . it's truly Tomatomania in the garden. My kind of tomato plant.

Pinch and Plant If you're removing larger side branching and have the room for more plants, you can easily and successfully "root," or plant, tomato cuttings. Here's how: Snip off a side branch that is at least six inches long. Put it in a vase or glass filled with water, and set the glass in a bright, but not brutally sunny, window for a few days. If you left it there for a couple of weeks, roots would appear along the stem, but you don't have to wait for that. Go ahead and "plant it out," after four or five days, burying most of the stem as you did with your other seedlings at planting time.

Water well, and keep that new plant more moist than the rest of the tomato garden for a couple of weeks (we're back to those first few watering weeks with this little guy). For best results, shade the cutting somehow from the hottest sun of the day.

The new cutting will likely droop and complain at first, and you'll think that you've lost it. Don't give up. Keep watering. The cuttings will generally come around in less than a week, and you're on your way to a brand-new plant. Remove the sun shade, but do continue to keep an eye on this one. It's still young compared to the other plants in your garden.

❧ A Stake to the Heart of the Matter ❧

Whether you pinch or not, the garden reality is that you will soon be challenged with a larger, heavier plant. It will begin to lean, then lean more, and if not attended to, eventually spread out on the ground all over your zucchini, beans, the porch, the driveway, and the rest of the summer garden. If you're growing on a hillside, this might be what you're after. But most of us will want to stop that intrusion by gathering and supporting the main stem and subsequent growth with a sturdy stake, cage, or other support.

[Cages are meant to support the core of the plant.]

Staking or caging is a space saver and keeps the plant up off the ground and out of your way. It allows better air circulation around the foliage, and upright foliage offers shade to developing fruit below. Stakes and cages also make it just a little harder for insects, critters, and even some soil-borne diseases to get access to your plant. All good things.

A word to the wise: Opt for heavy-duty stakes and cages if you have a choice.

TOMATO 101:

Just *hold it up!* The material or structure you use to support your plants truly isn't important. Anything strong enough to stand up under a huge fruiting beefsteak tomato in August makes a great tomato support. And hey, that's not a small feat. Function is key, but there are many attractive, inventive, and practical ways to keep your tomatoes off the ground. Be creative!

[Cage]

⁙ Cages ⁙

You're probably familiar with the standard tomato cage of light metal: larger circumference at the top and smaller down at the bottom. You place this over your plant and the plant grows up through it, spreading out and supporting itself as it presses against the ribs of the cage.

While there are many variations on that theme, this has been the most practical method for many gardeners for many years. For smaller determinates, this works just fine. If the plant is really large, caging packs branching too tightly together (not always a good thing in a more humid locale, or if disease may be afoot), and the farmer still must guide errant branching back into the confines of the cage as the season progresses.

❧ Stakes and Poles ❧

Cane or bamboo pole gardeners, you may start with one stake or pole, and end up with ten supporting the plant by season's end. Whatever works. Bamboo poles, tree stakes, metal piping, and anything similar will successfully hold up a tomato plant.

Sink the pole a few inches away from the stem. Don't worry about root damage, the plant will be fine. Tie the main stem to the stake as it grows, (loosely so as not to injure the stem) and employ additional poles as necessary to guide and support side branching.

Other options include tepees, which can also be made using poles, but they have always seemed to this gardener an odd choice. They are the opposite shape of the plant! But yes, they look really cool.

Now spirals, while they might seem silly or cute, are an engineering marvel. Their coils hold stems up extremely well. Know that they are best used when you pinch aggressively so that you have only one or two main stems of the plant to support. Another option: You could go crazy and use a dozen spirals to make a fanciful garden sculpture.

Ties That Bind . . . Attaching your plant to a stake or support is simple.

Use something soft and wide enough so it doesn't rip into the plant's stem as the branching gets heavier and heavier. Flexible plastic tie tape or wide-coated wire works well; heavy twine is good, too. My grandmother used old stockings or ripped up cotton T-shirts. But my favorite is good old-fashioned Velcro. Today, there is also a lighter "garden" version of the industrial-strength classic sold at many nurseries that works really well.

Tie off the main stem and largest branching to the stake first, being careful not to tie it too tightly. Attach lighter branching to separate stakes in the same way, as needed. Some gardeners will even support huge trusses of fruit with stakes, so they won't break off as they develop. This can be a good tactic if you're growing especially large fruit as well.

[No matter what you use as a stake,
Velcro is a good tying option.]

❧ Rigid Grids: Concrete Reinforcing Wire, Hog Wire, or Corral Fencing ❧

My favorite way to support tomato plants is a rigid grid that you can guide the plant through as it grows. No tying necessary. Concrete reinforcing wire is one grid option, and can be supported on posts as a panel or rolled into a cylinder to make a very strong, and I think rustically attractive, cage.

Livestock fencing (known as hog wire around my neck of the woods) sold in long panels works extremely well. Hog wire can be unwieldy to work with, but provides great support and the benefit of espalier-style growth. With the plant spread out on a plane in one layer, a larger percentage of leaves will get near-perfect sun exposure. Airflow is also maximized. The good folks at Kendall Jackson winery in Northern California grow tons of tomatoes each year on what used to be grape supports, essentially the same idea. Their production is phenomenal.

You can choose to support the grid in a vertical position, or lean it at an angle of forty-five to ninety degrees. The latter provides support underneath the plant, so your tomatoes will literally lie atop the grid, shading the growing fruit suspended underneath it. This method takes up a good bit of space, but you can use the shadier section underneath for lettuces or similar produce. And it's a great garden conversation piece.

[A quick tap helps increase your pollination percentage!]

⸙ Shake, Shake, Shake . . . ⸙

No matter what kind of support you are using, shaking your plants is a clever way to maximize your production throughout the season. A tomato plant doesn't need bees or other insects to act as a pollinator. In fact, the structure of the tomato flower allows it to self-pollinate quite easily. To encourage more self-pollinating (and more fruit) give this a try: On days when you see *a lot* of yellow flowers in the garden, walk through your plantings with a short length of pipe, rebar, or a piece of wood, and rap your stakes or supports lightly a few times. Yes, you might look a bit silly, and don't get crazy here and break branching, but try it! Agitating the flowers in this manner loosens pollen that will fertilize more flowers.

I once had a gardener in one of my classes tell me that she holds an electric toothbrush against the stems of her plants to accomplish this task. Whatever works. Just please, please don't use dental floss to tie up your plants!

Double Take Look around the garden and think creatively. What did you miss? Those posts that support your covered porch could be a tomato stake. Will they get enough sun there? The arbor over the path to the garage? Absolutely. That old swing set, or (no longer loved) play structure? The back fence? Yes, and yes. Use what you've already got in place.

The Garden Doctor Is *Out*

Dealing with critters and other challenges in the tomato garden

What bug?

As summer arrives, the first of many assaults might begin in your garden. Aphids arrive early, seeking fat new growth, spider mites love the hot dry parts of late summer, and hornworms love all seasons. *Arghhhh!*

You're growing tomatoes. You'll have challenges. Bugs love tomatoes, too, and although that plant label promises it is disease resistant, none are bullet proof. They may, in fact, succumb to one or more vascular diseases, bacterial infections, fungal infections, or random other pest infestations as the season progresses. Sounds like an ER ward, right? Some years, you will fly through the season unmarked by this kind of tragedy. Other years, you'll feel as if you have a target on your back—as if you haven't so much planted a garden, as laid out a buffet (or Petri dish) for various sundry and distasteful characters and infections.

The reality is that tomato diseases are often hard to diagnose and even harder to combat. Unless, that is, you happen to be a scientist. Have you looked at pictures on the Web or in books, trying to diagnose what's happening in your garden? It can be very frustrating.

Nonetheless, in this section, we're going to look at what you *can* do when you find and identify problems. Thankfully, pistols and poison aren't your only options—completely eradicating *all* life from your garden is never a good idea. Let's step back and take a balanced, whole-garden approach to the season. You're a farmer now. Don't stress out! Let's be optimistic and approach this calmly.

[Critters will usually avoid unripe fruit, waiting for a tastier meal later in the season.]

❧ Garden Avoidance Issues

Okay, full disclosure. Most seasons, I'm in complete denial of tomato diseases and pests. Or maybe I should say that I'm in full denial about accurately identifying, and then being able to do anything about, occasional bug and disease problems. That's mainly because I grow five or six hundred tomato plants (what was I thinking?) a season.

Addressing a problem may mean a weekend's worth of, well, addressing the problem. There's so much else to do most weekends. I'm much more likely to remove a plant that's failing and in danger of infecting the whole lot, rather than trying to identify, then treat, and then beat the situation. But that's just me.

So here's your first option when you notice a real problem in the garden: Do as I do, and remove the problem plant in question. It's not a bad option if you're growing four or five of a prized variety (so you're covered). Prune with a shovel, as they say. But the situation can seem much more dire and alarming when you only have two plants on your back deck. Hey, I get it. You don't want to lose half your potential harvest, so let's dig in and take a closer look.

⋛ Plant Rx ⋚

Start by doing everything right. Many a disease problem can be traced back to what you did or didn't do as you set up and started your garden. And lacking that, the weather is always a great scapegoat when you are in tomato distress—blame the rain. (Or the haze that seemed to hang around all through June!) If you are following good growing practices, and your plants are healthy from the start, you've taken the first step toward a disease-resistant season. Pests will always seek out the weakest plant in the garden first, and disease will be more virulent if the plant is just not right.

I like to divide problems into two parts: those challenges you can see right before your eyes, and those that creep in unannounced, and suddenly your plant is all brown and crunchy. The former applies to pests of every size and shape, the latter, to most diseases.

What Tomato Variety Do Deer Avoid? The one with the chicken-wire cage all the way around it. I hate to ask who bought the house in the woods, but I'm pretty sure it wasn't the family of deer. This (or they) can be one of the most stubborn problems in any garden. And these days, it seems more and more gardeners must tackle this issue. A *really* tall deer fence is a good alternative to handing out free suppers all summer. *Really* tall.

[Be alert! The signs of hornworms appear before major damage.]

❧ Pest Therapy ❧

We will all have to deal with pests in our tomato lifetimes. As you detect problems, know this: One grasshopper does not a plague make. And don't underestimate what you can do with a generous blast of water. The hose solves many pest problems in the garden. Just spray that grasshopper right *off* your plants. And keep spraying until you see that bug go . . . well, elsewhere.

And a little bit of insect insight: Ever wonder why the aphids you spray off your plants don't crawl right back up on the tomatoes and continue to wreck your weekend plans? It's true that when you spray aphids off your plants, since they are sucking on the plant, as aphids do, they are in fact separated from their mandibles. No, it's not a pretty idea, but it does solve your problem.

Here are a few other ways I've learned to cope with some of the most prevalent pest challenges over the years.

TOMATO HORNWORM ISSUES?

Yes, hornworms, like the magician at your tenth birthday party, can make your plants disappear in no time at all. Little black dots (frass, or hornworm poop) on the tops of leaves is a sign you'd better be vigilant. Don't freak out. Find them—the hard part given their camouflage—and dispose of them. They make a great lunch for chickens and local birds. (Adding a bird feeder to your garden might invite birds to do some of your dirty work.)

Bt, a naturally occurring bacillus used to prevent caterpillars on leaf crops, will get them, but must be used early. Hornworms are more active at night, so get out your flashlight and concentrate your search on the newer foliage on top of plants. Here's a pantry solution: They can't digest cornmeal, and they will be dispatched when they make the attempt. Spread cornmeal around both the base of the plants and on the leaves up higher. *If all else fails, offer your neighbor's kid a buck a worm and request daily reconnaissance missions.*

BEETLE HORROR FLICK IN THE MAKING?

While I've thankfully never had the pleasure of meeting a Colorado potato beetle, I have heard plenty of horror stories from Colorado and elsewhere. Your best defense, and also a good defense against the previously mentioned hornworm, by the way, is Bt. No, that's not a typo. *Bacillus thuringiensis* is a naturally occurring organism that will soon turn those pests into beetle juice. Bt is most often sold as a concentrate that you mix and then apply as a spray. Good to keep in the garden shed.

As with most pest problems, which do tend to be cyclical in many gardens, if you see one or two beetles, you can relax as they will likely do little damage. Get those out of there anyway, though. If you see two hundred (of *anything*!), it might be wise to take a different stance.

BIRDS EATING YOUR TOMATOES?

They're often just thirsty. Try adding a bird bath in the garden. You may even get a bonus: the birds stop eating your fruit and focus on their real goal, pudgy caterpillars and those hornworms. Netting or screening can work if the screen is suspended well above and around the plant. Otherwise birds will just land on the new perch you've constructed and continue to enjoy your harvest.

SQUIRREL ISSUES?

I'm convinced the whole *world* has squirrel issues. Those little buggers are aggressive. While dog and cat patrols can help, screening *completely* is your best defense against these and similar furry marauders. Set up traps, maybe the kind that "has a heart," at least initially. And, in case you really do have a heart and don't want to dispatch them, I won't officially advocate releasing them on your cranky ex-boss's property. Be aware though that in many areas it's illegal to transport such an animal (in order to get back at your boss). Even city and county governments hate squirrels!

GRASSHOPPERS CAMPING OUT BY YOUR PLANTS?

Catch them if you can. Use the hose to scare them away. There's truly not much you can do, other than cover your plants with poison. Definitely *not* a good option.

SLOW, BUT STICKY, MOVERS MOVING IN?

Snails and slugs will do a surprisingly good job of making one tiny hole in a tomato for themselves, thereby ruining the fruit for you. Catch them with beer traps (the ones that party), or line your planting area with copper tape to keep the slimy guys at bay. New organic snail baits are also effective, but you must apply those regularly. And don't forget to use that in the ivy adjacent to the veggie garden!

If you're using hay as mulch, a word to the wise: While good at keeping soil temperatures in the lower register, mulch is a wonderful home for slugs and snails. Two inches of mulch is good, eight inches is a snail condo.

Tomato 911 Tomato pests come in many forms. Some chase cats and answer to Rover, as illustrated by this e-mail I got a few years ago that still makes me smile (and I'm paraphrasing here):

"I just came home to find that my Labrador ate all the tomatoes in my garden. Juice is running down his chin. Honestly, I'm not sure whether to be angry or jealous!"

Pups can be Tomatomaniacs, too! If you're still not convinced, I'd be happy to share the video of my Australian shepherd eating cherry tomatoes right off my plants. So yes, it would be wise to protect your freshly picked, or almost ready to be picked, fruit from furry friends.

[Most gardeners can expect a very tired-looking plant at the end of the season. Wouldn't you be, too?]

"Tools" for the Shed Who knows what challenges might await in your garden? Be ready with organic options to deal with insect infestations. Horticultural oil is one piece of ammunition that you should always have on hand, as are organic sprays that contain pyrethrins, an effective pest combatant.

Insecticidal soaps (and various other home remedies that are all over the Web) have a place in this arsenal as well. With organic products, you will need to be more diligent and may have to repeat applications more frequently than with the other pseudo-nuclear products on the market, but do it. The vegetable garden is your last stand against chemicals in your food. Take advantage of that. If, and when, you find unwelcome characters, you know what to do next: Follow the directions on the label. And crossing your fingers can't hurt, either.

❧ The Yellow Leaves of Our Lives ❧

Yes, managing maladies can feel like a soap opera sometimes. I can document many a frantic trip to the local nursery when a good gardener sees yellowing tomato leaves. There's no need to be so dramatic, though, as a change in leaf color does *not* necessarily signal the imminent demise of your plant(s).

As lower leaves become ineffective, the plant will often slough them off (they get no sun, so they can't produce food for the plant). Those leaves turn yellow. Just cut them off and get them out of the garden. And just in case there are undesirables of any kind there, don't add the leaves to your compost pile. Now, if the yellowing appears suddenly and progresses rapidly, and you find curious spots or creatures upon closer inspection, you might make that trip (put the leaf in a plastic bag, please!) to a local nursery to get first-hand assistance.

❧ The Invisible Threat ❧

When people call or write me in plant panic mode, by far the most asked questions is, *"Help! I have spots all over my plants."* I wish it was a simple problem to answer. If a grasshopper did in fact visit the garden yesterday, its enthusiastic chewing may bruise the plant, causing holes and often spots or bruised sections, too. Diseases that are soil borne (vascular, fungal, or bacterial) will cause spotting of various kinds on leaves and stems. *A lot of things* cause spots on leaves, and yes, that's frustrating.

EARLY AND LATE BLIGHT

Early and late blight are culprits that will cause spotting and are unfortunately one of the most common diseases you may fight in the tomato garden. Plants can grow and produce through early blight. That is not true of late blight, which is not curable. The fruit will be blemished and misshapen and will have to be discarded. There's not much you can do to prevent either; it's the luck of the garden draw, as they say. However, you should keep your garden clean and remove any leaves that begin to show signs of disease. If you're growing potatoes in the garden, I hate to break it to you, but yes, it's probably a good idea to get rid of them, too. Late blight is persistent in potato roots and tubers.

WILT

Wilt might also cause spotting. But it's more likely that if your plants suffer from this malady, they will droop and then turn brown and crunchy in short order. If you're gardening in a cooler climate and you get wilt, you're probably dealing with verticillium wilt. In warmer areas, fusarium wilt might be the culprit at hand. These are often impossible to accurately diagnose, and consequently, to treat. Your best defense is often to remove those plants immediately. Get ready to move the garden next year!

The great tomato books and online resources that are mentioned on page 199 in the Resources section offer a much more detailed assessment of the kinds of diseases that will attack your plants. I want to mention Mike McGrath's *You Bet Your Garden Guide to Growing Great Tomatoes,* also. It offers a chuckle or a hearty belly laugh, even when dealing with dire garden situations, along with his good advice. We're all lucky to have these resources.

The Theory of (Harvest) Relativity

Disease, what disease? If tragedy strikes, don't be hard on yourself. This stuff happens to farmers. It's the natural cycle of plant life. And while on this topic, let's take just a moment to tip our hats to all those who till the soil, grow food, and feed us for a living. Their devotion and work ethic is something we only have the faintest glimpse of as we start our backyard gardens. Imagine for a minute if solving bug or disease problems was the key to your income and family security. Yikes. Thank you, farmers.

Hello, Summer! When it gets really, really hot, protect your plants! Mulch heavily (again) under your plants to maintain cool soil temperatures. This will insulate the soil, but it also helps keep disease spores or affected soil particles from being splashed up onto your plants. Mulch the driveway around your containers to protect those pots from reflected heat. Really! It will help immensely.

If mulch on the driveway seems silly, wrap your pots for the same reason. The exterior of a container can get extremely hot in the summer, which subsequently causes the entire pot to become way too warm. Roots grow quickly and will circle around the interior of the container right against the pot. Guess what gets fried first? Your goal is to keep the roots *cool*, just as they would be if you planted them in the ground. Use burlap or something similar so you can water and feed right through it.

And remember, be sure to check the sprinkler system to make sure all is well there and the water is being applied wisely.

[A few inches of mulch gets the job done.
Eight inches? Now you've got a snail condo.]

⁍ Could Something (Someone!) Else Be the Problem? ⁌

It's true, sometimes the problem in the garden is neither disease nor insect. Are you seeing a lot of flowers but no fruit yet? Cool nights and other environmental factors may be telling the plant that the time is not yet right to bear fruit. More often, it's caused by things we can control.

If the plant is stressed by insects, that's one thing, and if it's getting too little water, that's an easy thing to fix.

But maybe it's getting way too much water or fertilizer. Are you the only person in your household who waters the tomatoes? Could it be you're living with a softie who's doing a little irrigating or fertilizing on the side? (Okay, who *else* has the key to the garden shed?) Either situation can result in the plant delaying the onset of fruit. Step back and take a closer look at how you—and those in your household—are managing the basics!

⁍ When to Throw in the Shovel ⁌

The good news, after all this depressing stuff, is that most tomato plants can get through a bug infestation or even a bout with early blight, for example, and still offer you some tomatoes in return for your time and energy. Don't run up the white flag too early.

However, sometimes, you've just got to let it go. Do it. Prune with that shovel. I know it's hard, but there will be other seasons. Promise.

But hey, that doesn't mean you can't start over again with new plants or those cuttings you started in a different section of the garden! You might just get lucky and redeem your season.

[Remember, diseased plant material does NOT go in the compost pile.]

You Didn't Just Pick that Tomato . . .
Did You?

Waiting for the right moment to harvest your crop

OK, no harm, no foul. We've got a plan.

If you're one of the lucky gardeners who have the luxury of watching your tomatoes fully ripen on the vine we'll help be right on time for the rest of the season. Yes, it is hard to wait.

Some of you will absolutely have to pick early (see The Critter Exception, page 127), but that's not the end of the world. Just don't eat it right away. Let fruit that's too firm sit for a bit. It will wow you later. Or you could pop it into a First Pick Hand Pie (see page 129). Just sayin'!

❧ The Ripeness Game ❧

Hands down, the biggest advantage you have as a home gardener is the opportunity to watch gorgeous tomatoes ripen on the vine and pick them when they are ultimately *ripe!*

Seems like a silly concept, right? Too easy. Who's gonna pick a tomato before it's ripe? Well, we all do—just not on purpose.

Consider this: Some commercial tomatoes are picked green, trucked to warehouses, and gassed with ethylene so they will color up and look like the fruit that is ripening in your garden. Nothing could be more unnatural, but given shipping requirements and the sheer magnitude of supplying all of us with tomatoes year-round, well, that's how it's done. Lucky us.

At home, you won't be blasting your tomatoes with gas, but as they begin to ripen there is always the temptation to pick your crop too early. When you do pick and eat fruit early, you can wind up with much less flavorful tomatoes. You can avoid that by allowing your fruit to ripen fully on the plant. The rewards will be *oh so much* greater. This is the difference between homegrown tomato taste and those . . . other guys.

Green Tomato Envy

There are green tomatoes, and then there are green tomatoes. Green Zebra, Green Doctors, Aunt Ruby's German Green, and Spear's Tennessee Green are all tomatoes that will be green in color when they are completely ripe. You already know that every tomato is green before it begins to turn its ultimate color.

So, how do you know when a green variety is ripe? Greens will generally "blush" with chartreuse or a yellowish hue when ripe. There's your indicator. A green light to pick, of sorts.

[Ananas Noire (Black Pineapple), a stunning green heirloom.]

One variety at different stages of ripeness. Patience is everything.

Shades of Red . . . or Yellow, Orange, Green, or Purple

Each tomato will exhibit a natural progression of color, from green and unripe to fully colored. Of course, this progression of shades depends on what color the tomato variety will ultimately be. Red tomatoes generally turn slightly peach or orange, then rosy, and finally ripen to a wonderful shade of red. Wait another day or two, and you will see them turn an even *deeper* red! That's what you want. I know this is hard to do, but *wait*. This is *especially* important with smaller and early varieties.

Granted, the color changes may not always be so obvious. You may not know how to tell when a black tomato is ripe until you've seen that happen for a season (many turn a deep plum or chocolate color), but the key to picking those, and all tomatoes in your garden, is the same. The fruit needs to be bright, fully colored and (you're still waiting, not picking, right?), softening. Firm fruit is simply not yet ripe.

⋛ The Softer Side of Summer ⋚

Every tomato, no matter the size, color, name, or country of origin, will begin to soften when it is fully ripe. Fess up. We all squeeze tomatoes (and other fruits and veggies) in the supermarket. If you want to use it for dinner tonight, that tomato has to be soft, not firm, right? The same goes for homegrown tomatoes. The fruit arcs through the ripening pattern we've just talked about, and then after turning its deepest color, the tomato begins to "give" a little when you pick it up.

Granted, it is *much* easier to be patient at the end of the season when there are piles of tomatoes on the counter. I can't tell you how many times I hear 'maniacs tell me that "short-season" varieties just don't taste good. They're actually great tomatoes, we just get excited and tend to pick and eat them too early! As plants get larger and the first fruit begins to grow, many of us will peer longingly out the kitchen window every fifteen minutes until we see what we're *convinced* is ripe fruit on our plants. We race out to the garden, check over the fence (quickly!) to make sure we are the first in the neighborhood to harvest, and eagerly snag that blur of red or yellow or black. Back in the kitchen, much to our chagrin, we bite into a decent, but not great, tomato. False start.

Reality check: Smaller early tomatoes and late-season beefsteaks are definitely not the same animal, so don't expect them to taste the same. If truly ripe, both will taste terrific, but a leopard can't change its spots. So wait patiently for that first Stupice, Ida Gold, or Golden Mama to ripen. Enjoy your first pick simply with a sprinkle of fine sea salt, or maybe in the first tomato salad of the season. Summer has arrived. Use it! Cook it! Enjoy it!

[Spoon]

❧ The Critter Exception ❧

Yes, I'm advocating that you leave your tomatoes on the plant for as long as possible. But here's the thing: You're not the only one waiting anxiously for that fruit to ripen (funny how squirrels, raccoons, and other wildlife know what's going on in your garden plot). As we already talked about, some gardeners will completely enclose or cage their plants to combat this onslaught. That's a big job, though, and often simply impossible to do anyway.

If critters are enjoying all your Brandywines and leaving none for you, it's better to pick just a little early than to pick nothing at all. When you notice the first color "break," when the shoulders of the fruit start to really color, go ahead and pick. Cut it off the plant, don't rip it, so you won't tear the flesh. Put that fruit in a cool, dark place (no, not in a sunny window), and you should get very representative, true tomato flavor when it finishes coloring up.

But . . . if you did pick a little out of turn, and you're holding tomatoes that you've now determined need a few days to ripen, don't fret. Make the most of them in First Pick Hand Pies (page 129).

You can use any tomato variety, as long as they are firm and immature (unripe). This also works wonderfully at the end of the season, when that first frost threat sneaks up on you while there are still loads of fruit on your plants. Wait and use a soft tomato for these pies, and you're too late. A reversal of tomato fortune.

First Pick Hand Pies

Makes 6 pies

Tomato soup cake, that classic 1930s spice cake (inspired by a certain soup company) is a dessert that people love—or love to hate. It made frequent appearances at Sam's grandmother's house as Mystery Cake, what most folks called it back then (she claimed that if she called it tomato cake, the kids would never have eaten it). It's still a favorite at our house and at our tomato tastings.

Regardless of where you stand on canned-soup issues, these walnut- and raisin-filled hand pies packed with first-picked tomatoes of the season, quick-candied ginger, citrus, and spices are a whole other homegrown pastry altogether. Baking the pies in cupcake liners make them portable, so I find myself doing a lot of "essential" early tomato pruning (from Sam's vines, of course) throughout the summer and into the fall. Save the syrup from the candied ginger to use in summer libations such as iced tea, lemonade, and cocktails. And be sure to raise a glass to Grandma Hamann.

Note: You can substitute homemade candied orange peel instead of ginger. Store-bought versions of both also work well.

PIE CRUST

16 tablespoons (2 sticks) unsalted butter, cut into ½-inch pieces and frozen for 10 minutes

2½ cups all-purpose flour

¼ teaspoon salt

1 teaspoon white vinegar

⅓ to ½ cup ice water

(continued)

TO MAKE THE PIE CRUST:

1. Place the butter, flour, and salt in a food processor and pulse quickly 10 times (I like to put a kitchen towel over the processor to catch flour dust), until the mixture resembles a coarse cornmeal with some pea-sized pieces of butter. (You can also place the dry ingredients in a large bowl and lightly rub the butter between your fingers.)

2. Open the food processor to pour the vinegar and ⅓ cup of ice water over the dough to evenly distribute both. Pulse 2 or 3 more times, just until the liquid is incorporated. Turn the dough out into a large bowl. If the dough is too dry to pinch together with your hands, add additional ice water, 1 tablespoon at a time, just until it holds together loosely.

(continued)

PIE FILLING

4 cups (about 2 pounds) firm "first picks" (unripe, green) tomatoes, chopped into ¼-inch pieces

½ cup packed dark brown sugar

½ cup plus 1 tablespoon granulated sugar, divided

2 tablespoons all-purpose flour

1 teaspoon orange zest, packed (from about 1 medium orange)

1 teaspoon ground cinnamon

½ teaspoon freshly grated nutmeg

½ teaspoon ground cloves

⅛ teaspoon kosher salt

½ cup raisins

½ cup toasted walnuts, roughly chopped

¼ cup finely chopped candied ginger, store bought or homemade (recipe follows)

2 teaspoons vegetable oil or nonstick cooking spray

3. Form the dough into two approximately 6 x 4-inch rectangles. Wrap in plastic wrap and refrigerate at least one hour or overnight.

TO MAKE THE PIE FILLING:

1. Spread out the tomatoes on kitchen or paper towels to drain.

2. Mix together the brown sugar, ½ cup granulated sugar, flour, orange zest, cinnamon, nutmeg, cloves, salt, raisins, walnuts, and candied ginger in a large bowl. Use your fingers to make sure the ginger is mixed in well. Gently fold in the tomatoes.

TO ASSEMBLE THE PIES:

1. Preheat the oven to 375°F and place a rack in the middle of the oven. Stack 6 paper cupcake liners together and use scissors to trim the sides so they are about ½-inch tall. Repeat with another 6 cupcake liners. Lightly coat a 12-cup standard muffin tin with nonstick cooking spray or a neutral cooking oil, place the cupcake liners in each tin, and lightly coat the inside of the liners with spray or oil.

2. On a lightly floured work surface, roll one dough rectangle into a rectangle roughly 16 x 8 inches. Use a pastry cutter or knife to cut the dough horizontally in half, then into 3 sections vertically to make 6 squares (if the dough breaks in a few places, that's fine). I like a few rough edges, but you can trim the squares if that's your thing. Nestle each square of dough into a muffin cup, leaving the overhang on the

edges. Pinch the edges together in a few places and patch any holes in the bottom with dough scraps. Repeat with the remaining dough. Refrigerate the muffin tins for 10 minutes.

3. Divide the tomato filling among each muffin cup, filling them almost to the top. Sprinkle the pies with the remaining tablespoon of granulated sugar. Place a baking sheet on the bottom rack of the oven to catch any drippings and bake for 20 minutes. Reduce the heat to 350°F, rotate the pan from front to back, and bake until the pie crusts are lightly golden brown and the filling is set, 25 to 30 minutes.

4. Place the muffin tin on a wire rack to cool. After 20 minutes, run a knife around the edges to loosen any caramelized bits stuck to the sides of the pan. Allow the pies to cool completely before removing from tins.

CANDIED GINGER

About ½ pound ginger, peeled

1 cup sugar

1. Slice the ginger into very thin coins. Pull off and discard any stringy bits. Place the ginger and enough water to cover in a small saucepan, bring to a boil, and drain.

2. In the same saucepan, bring the blanched ginger, sugar, and 1 cup of water to a boil. Stir to dissolve the sugar, reduce the heat, and simmer until ginger is tender when pierced with a knife, 15 to 20 minutes, depending on the thickness of the slices. Remove from the heat and set aside to cool completely. Refrigerate candied ginger in syrup for up to 1 month, or strain (reserve the syrup for another use) and toss the candied pieces in granulated sugar.

Let's *Eat!*

Recipes and kitchen tips

My Favorite Tomato Recipe

Rigorously tested countless times. Foolproof. Pick a ripe, beautifully colored, and slightly soft tomato off the vine. The only thing better than trying this with one perfectly ripe, juicy tomato? Trying it with ten perfectly ripe tomatoes of different colors and types. You're welcome!

WASH IT. (Or not.)

CUT IT. (Or not.)

SALT IT. (Or not.)

EAT IT. (Best done outdoors.)

Sure, many of you will eliminate the salt-it step and that's fine with me. You've worked really hard to get to this step and final product. Don't miss the opportunity to savor the basic essence of this crop you've grown in your own backyard. Dive right in!

⊰ Scott's Golden (or Red, Green, Orange) Tomato Kitchen Rules ⊱

ANY HOMEGROWN TOMATO IS A GREAT TOMATO FOR ANY DISH.
Sure, certain varieties work better in some recipes, like a juicier variety in gazpacho. But we're talking about *homegrown* tomatoes. They're all fantastic, all the time. You can always mix and match varieties.

USE *EVERY* LAST BIT OF *EVERY* TOMATO.
I take this literally, down to the seeds and skin. I like the texture contrast. I know some people can't eat the seeds. If this is you, definitely toss them in the compost bin. And sure, skins can look a bit funny and add a unique texture to cooked dishes, but I leave them in. Puree if you must. I encourage you to try this experiment: Bake one tomato whole and bake another one that has been stripped of seeds and skin. Take a bite of each. Taste the difference? The seeds in particular have more umami-inducing glutamic acid (fancy, right?), so they pack in a whole lot of flavor.

NEVER REFRIGERATE TOMATOES.
I urge you to become refrigerator-resistant Tomatomaniacs, even in the softest hours. Refrigeration destroys the delicate aromatic essences and flavor-packed membranes in the flesh and makes tomatoes mealy and tasteless. When your tomatoes split or get too soft, you can always freeze them. Freeze? Yes.

WHEN IN DOUBT, *FREEZE.*
My grandfather tossed his tomatoes in a freezer the size of his trusty Dodge every year. These tomatoes made the best winter tomato sauce ever. Thawed tomatoes are squishy, yes (the cell membranes break down), and definitely not salad material. But unlike refrigeration, freezing preserves a tomato's flavor, so they're perfect for soups, sauces, and pretty much anything in a sauté pan. And here, if you're not a fan of the skin, it slips right off frozen tomatoes after they thaw.

Sure, you can slice and bag tomatoes. But to save time, freeze them whole. I even know people who don't use a bag!

⁕ Kitchen Basics ⁕

PEELING AND SEEDING

To peel: Cut a small, shallow X in the bottom of each tomato. Carefully drop the tomatoes all at once into a large pot of simmering water, strain after thirty seconds to avoid cooking them, and immediately plunge the tomatoes into an ice bath. The skin should easily peel off, starting at the X.

To remove the seeds: Simply squeeze—okay that's messy—or scoop the seeds out with your finger or a spoon. See how easy that is? If you're pureeing the tomatoes, you can push the pulp through a chinois or other fine-mesh strainer.

TOMATO WATER

All that great clear juice inside the tomato cavity has a subtle but distinct tomato flavor, very different from store-bought juice. Use tomato water to poach seafood and chicken, blanch vegetables, or as a cocktail base (see Black Martini, page 145).

To save tomato water: As you chop tomatoes, dump any juice that accumulates on your cutting board directly into a bowl, easy as that. Anytime you smash tomatoes, as in the Mediterranean Smash (page 157), use a colander-lined bowl to catch the drippings. Store tomato water in the fridge for up to five days or freeze.

TOP OF THE POT STOCK

The liquid that lingers at the top of bubbling pots of tomatoes on the stove is one of my favorite ways to sneak a little tomato flavor into *everything*. It also cuts down on the time it takes for the liquid to reduce when you are making large batches of fresh tomato-based sauces and soups.

To make Top of the Pot Stock: When you simmer a large pot of tomatoes for canning, soup, or sauce, periodically skim off a portion of the liquid that separates from the tomatoes (see Tomato Sauce recipe, page 164, for details). When I'm making big batches of sauce and soup, I keep a bowl of stock in the fridge for a few days and keep adding to it. All of the spices and flavorings from whatever I am cooking blend together to make a rich vegetable stock.

Freeze Top of the Pot Stock in freezer bags or an ice cube tray for smaller deglazing portions (pop out the cubes and store in freezer bags). Use the stock in Sam's Tomato Sourdough (page 173) as a soup base, to deglaze a pan instead of wine, or toss it into any winter dish in need of a summer flavor boost.

OVEN-DRIED TOMATOES

Have you ever tried drying cherry tomatoes on the dashboard of your car on a hot summer day? Your ride will smell like Luigi's pizza parlor for a week, but trust me, it works. (Best avoided on carpool days.)

The amount of baking time required to dry tomatoes varies depending on the variety, size, and ripeness of your tomatoes. Peanut brittle is not the end game. The tomatoes are "dry" when shriveled but still springy to the touch.

To make oven-dried tomatoes: Preheat the oven to 200°F. Halve any small tomatoes and slice large tomatoes into two- to three-inch wedges. Place the tomatoes, cut-side up, in a single layer on a lightly oiled baking sheet. Sprinkle lightly with salt and roast until the tomatoes are dry but still springy to the touch, as few as three hours for cherry tomatoes and up to seven hours for larger, juicy tomatoes. Cool completely and refrigerate, completely covered in olive oil, for up to two weeks. To freeze, spread the dried tomatoes (without oil) in a single layer on a baking sheet. When frozen, pluck them off individually and store in a freezer bag.

My Not-So-Secret Kitchen Secret: Tony Chachere's Original Creole Seasoning

Tony Chachere was a Louisiana legend and a businessman who loved to cook. He started a successful food company after he retired. His grandson runs the business today.

Like Tony, the spice runs thick in my Louisiana bloodline. Today, like most of my family and friends, I order his Original Creole Seasoning by the gallon-sized tub (all seven pounds of it!) and add the spicy blend to *everything*: roasted and baked tomatoes, sauces, soups, eggs, you name it. In my kitchen, this spicy and secret combo never misses. If there is something tomato-based bubbling on my stove, you can bet it's got a hefty dash of this Creole seasoning in it.

These days you can order Tony Chachere's Original Creole Seasoning directly from the Web site and find it at many grocery stores.

Black Martini

Some people swear a martini should only be served neat; others like to "dirty" things up with olive juice. I'm pretty sure neither has tried Sam's spicy version made with the freshly squeezed juice of homegrown tomatoes.

You can use any tomatoes in this cocktail, but if you happen to have a few black varieties lingering on the bar counter like Black Krim or Black Ethiopian, they make a mean-looking martini.

2 tablespoons freshly squeezed tomato water (see page 140), from a black tomato variety if you have one, chilled

2 dashes Tabasco or other hot sauce

2 dashes Worcestershire sauce

1 tablespoon freshly squeezed lemon juice, lemon reserved

Pinch of kosher salt

Pinch of freshly ground black pepper

5 tablespoons good-quality vodka, such as Ketel One

A generous ½ teaspoon celery salt, to rim the glass

2 fresh or quick-pickled cherry tomatoes (page 148), for garnish

1. Place a martini glass in the freezer to chill for 5 minutes.

2. Mix together the tomato water, Tabasco, Worcestershire, lemon juice, salt, and pepper in a small glass.

3. Pour the vodka into an ice-filled cocktail shaker and shake or stir, whatever your preference (we know what Sean Connery would do), until the vodka is well chilled.

4. Sprinkle the celery salt on a small plate. Rub the reserved lemon around the rim. Turn the glass upside down and dip it in the salt to lightly coat the rim of the glass.

5. Strain the vodka into the chilled glass. Very slowly add the tomato water mixture so some of the liquid sinks to the bottom of the martini glass. Garnish with the cherry tomatoes and serve immediately.

Prime Picks: Any juicy heirloom varieties.

Best left on the vine: Meatier varieties, such as Romas or oxhearts. (Where's the juice?)

Tomato Sunrise

If you've ever had chips and salsa while sipping a margarita (and who hasn't?), you know that tequila and tomatoes complement each other. It works just as well in this tequila-based alternative to a traditional Bloody Mary using Top of the Pot Stock. If you're brunching to impress, the cocktail is prettiest if the stock is made from yellow tomatoes.

3 tablespoons good-quality blanco tequila (also known as silver)

½ cup Top of the Pot Stock (page 140), preferably made with yellow tomato varieties, room temperature

1 tablespoon fresh lemon juice

½ teaspoon soy sauce

¼ teaspoon freshly grated or jarred horseradish

3 dashes garlicky chili sauce, such as Sriracha, or to taste

Sprig of cilantro

1. Place a highball glass in the freezer to chill for 5 minutes.

2. Combine the tequila, Top of the Pot Stock, lemon juice, soy sauce, horseradish, and chili sauce in an ice-filled cocktail shaker. Shake thoroughly until well chilled, about 10 seconds. Season with additional chili sauce to taste.

3. Strain the mixture into the chilled glass. Garnish with cilantro and serve immediately.

Prime Picks: Any combination of yellow tomato variety will make great stock. Don't cook it too long or it will turn brown.

Best left on the vine: Pass on meatier, drier Roma-types.

Quick Pickled Spoons

Makes 1 cup

A chef in Los Angeles once asked me to find the tiniest tomato to use as a garnish, the sort of thing Gulliver would have plucked from vines in Lilliput (or thousands of years ago in Peru, where native tomatoes were initially the size of berries).

Turns out, the fruit on my World's Smallest Tomato (yes, there is such a variety) plant was bigger than Spoons, the tiniest tomato variety I'd ever grown. Picking pea-sized Spoons can be a labor of love, but they have such a great sweet-tart flavor, it's pretty impossible not to keep diving back in.

Make sure the brine is cool before marinating the tomatoes, and brine them only briefly, so the tomatoes keep their bright flavor and firm texture. To make more of a relish-style pickle, substitute any juicy, well-drained, finely diced tomato.

1 cup (about 6 ounces) firm cherry, grape, or other small tomatoes

½ cup cider vinegar

2 teaspoons sugar

2 teaspoons kosher salt

One 2-inch piece fresh ginger, peeled and thinly sliced

½ serrano or jalapeño pepper, seeded

One 3-inch sprig fresh rosemary

1 teaspoon whole yellow mustard seeds or ½ teaspoon mustard powder

1. Wash and thoroughly dry the tomatoes on paper towels and place them in a 2-cup glass measuring cup or small, deep glass bowl.

2. Combine the vinegar, sugar, salt, ginger, serrano or jalapeño pepper, rosemary, and mustard seeds in a small saucepan. Bring the mixture to a boil for 30 seconds, remove from the heat, and set aside to cool completely.

3. Pour the cooled vinegar mixture over the tomatoes, making sure the tomatoes are completely submerged (remove the rosemary and a few slices of ginger if necessary). Marinate for 30 minutes or up to 1 hour, drain, and serve immediately.

Prime picks: Any cherry, grape, or other small, firm tomatoes for small pickles. Juicy beefsteaks for relish.

Best left on the vine: Less juicy stuffer and Roma-type varieties.

Tomato–Vanilla Bean Marmalade

At our annual end-of-season Tomatomania tasting in L.A., Southern California 'maniacs bring their gems of the season to share. After we taste *every* homegrown tomato (a hard job, I know), chef and fellow 'maniac Jimmy Shaw prepares an incredible tomato-inspired brunch. At some point, the tomato-doused conversation always seems to circle back to tomato relishes, ketchups, and jams like this marmalade-style tomato preserve with vanilla beans.

The two ingredients may seem like unlikely kitchen friends, but go with me for a second; this recipe is well worth the vanilla bean splurge. The marmalade is fantastic on breakfast toast, piled on goat cheese–topped crusty bread, or crackers for a quick lunch or appetizer, or swirled into tangy frozen yogurt as a nightcap—just my kind of all-day tomato tasting.

Note: To make the jam with frozen tomatoes, reduce the sugar to ½ cup plus 2 tablespoons sugar (they lose juice when thawed). Thawed tomato skins slip off easily, so the marmalade will have a smoother, more jamlike consistency.

3 pounds very ripe, sweet tomatoes, blemishes and rough spots removed

¾ cup sugar

½ vanilla bean, scraped

Generous pinch of kosher salt

1. Cut the stem end off the tomatoes and remove any tough cores. Scoop out half the seeds with your finger (a few left are fine). Place the tomatoes in a colander over a bowl and roughly smash them into 1-inch chunks with your hands. Discard any skins that slip off while you work. Reserve the tomato water for another use.

2. Place the strained tomatoes, sugar, vanilla bean and scrapings, and salt in a medium saucepan. Bring the mixture to a boil, reduce the heat to retain a low boil, and cook, stirring frequently, until the liquid has evaporated and the marmalade is glossy, 25 to 35 minutes, depending on the juiciness of the tomatoes. (The jam will thicken more as it cools.) Cool and refrigerate for up to 1 month.

(continued)

Note: This jam does not have enough acid to safely can and preserve.

Prime picks: Any sweet red or yellow tomatoes such as Thessaloniki, Lemon Boy, Early Girls, and bicolors similar to Pineapple.

Best left on the vine: Purple varieties often take on a muddy color when cooked; citrusy green varieties such as Garden Lime, Emerald Evergreen, and Green Moldovan don't pair well with vanilla.

Five-Minute Tomato–Vanilla Bean Frozen Yogurt

Combine 2 cups plain whole milk yogurt, ½ cup heavy whipping cream, 2 teaspoons fresh lemon juice, and ½ cup powdered sugar in a large bowl. Whisk until smooth. Freeze in an ice-cream maker according to the manufacturer's instructions. Swirl ⅓ cup Tomato–Vanilla Bean Marmalade (page 151) into the yogurt (don't overmix), and freeze for 1 to 2 hours. Serve immediately to prevent the yogurt from becoming icy.

Pineapple (Tomato) Upside-Down Cake

Makes 1 cake; 8 to 10 servings

Super sweet and citrusy tomatoes alike are pretty near perfect in this rustic cornmeal cake. Use bicolor yellow varieties splashed with streaks of red, such as sweet Pineapple tomatoes (you bet there is a Pineapple variety!) if you have them. Citrusy green tomatoes mellow a bit color-wise when baked, but are also fantastic.

1 pound (1 very large or two medium) very ripe, sweet tomatoes

8 tablespoons (1 stick) plus 3 tablespoons unsalted butter at room temperature, divided, plus more to butter the cake pan

½ cup dark brown sugar, packed

2 teaspoons orange zest, packed (about 1 medium orange), fruit reserved for juicing

1 teaspoon lemon zest, packed (about 1 medium lemon)

½ cup honey

2 large eggs, lightly beaten

½ cup sour cream

¼ cup freshly squeezed orange juice

¾ cup all-purpose flour

1 cup cornmeal

1½ teaspoons baking powder

½ teaspoon baking soda

¼ teaspoon kosher salt

Crème fraîche and honey, to serve (optional)

1. Preheat the oven to 350°F. Lightly butter a 9-inch round cake pan, line the bottom with parchment paper, and butter the paper. Slice the tomatoes ⅓ inch thick and spread them out on paper towels to drain.

2. Melt 3 tablespoons butter over medium-high heat in a small saucepan. Add the brown sugar and cook just until the sugar is melted, about 1 minute. Pour the brown sugar paste into the prepared cake pan and immediately spread it out as evenly as possible using a heat-proof spatula. Combine the orange and lemon zests and sprinkle 1 teaspoon over the top of the brown sugar.

3. Combine the remaining 8 tablespoons butter, honey, eggs, sour cream, orange juice, and remaining 2 teaspoons of orange-lemon zest in a stand mixer fitted with the paddle attachment and mix well. (Alternatively, use a hand mixer.) In a small bowl, whisk the flour, cornmeal, baking powder, baking soda, and salt, add the butter mixture, and mix until just combined.

(continued)

4. Blot any moisture off the tomatoes and arrange them decoratively in the bottom of the pan. (I like to leave a little space between the slices to see the patterns in each). Pour the batter over the tomatoes. Bake until the cake is lightly brown, starts to pull away from the sides, and a toothpick inserted in the middle comes out clean, 45 to 50 minutes. Allow the cake to cool in the pan on a wire rack for 20 minutes. Run a knife around the edges of the pan, place a serving plate on top, and (wearing oven mitts!), flip the cake onto the plate. Allow the cake to cool completely. To gild the lily, serve the cake with a dollop of crème fraîche and a drizzle of honey.

Prime picks: Sweet bicolors like Pineapple, Gold Medal, or Grandma Viney's Yellow Pink, or citrusy green varietiess such as Ananas Noire (Black Pineapple) or Aunt Ruby's German Green.

Mediterranean Smash

Makes about 2½ to 3 cups

Late in the summer in Buñol, Spain, locals dodge paste tomatoes instead of bulls at La Tomatina tomato festival. Basically, the cobblestone streets turn into a giant, slippery, tomato-covered slide. It's *crazy* fun. Slosh through smashed tomatoes and you very quickly appreciate both their virtues and their acidity in a whole new light. And yes, next time, I'll wear goggles like the seasoned pros.

This relish uses Spanish ingredients including sherry vinegar and smoked paprika, but you can use the same technique with any salsa, really. Super ripe "seconds" tomatoes are especially easy to smash. Really go for it when you mash the tomatoes to make a smoother salsa-like dip, or leave the salsa chunkier for a grilled fish, bean soup, or grilled crusty bread topping. Either way, the leftovers are great folded into quinoa salad. Smashed tomatoes continue to release their juice as they sit, so serve immediately.

2 pounds very ripe tomatoes, "seconds" work well, blemishes and rough spots removed

2 teaspoons sherry vinegar

2 teaspoons fresh lemon juice, more to taste

1 tablespoon extra-virgin olive oil

½ teaspoon smoked paprika

1 medium clove garlic, minced

¼ medium red onion, thinly sliced and roughly chopped

¼ cup good-quality, roughly chopped Mediterranean olives (green, black, or a mix)

½ cup loosely packed parsley, roughly chopped

Kosher salt

Freshly ground black pepper to taste

1. Place the tomatoes in a large bowl and smash them with your hands into ½-inch chunks. Discard any skin that comes off in the process. Place the tomatoes in a colander-lined bowl to drain. You should have about 2½ to 3 cups of tomato meat.

2. In another bowl, combine the sherry vinegar, lemon juice, olive oil, paprika, garlic, red onion, olives, and parsley. Toss the tomatoes with your hands to remove any accumulated juices in the colander and add the tomatoes to the sherry vinaigrette, leaving behind most of the seeds at the bottom of the colander. (Save the tomato water

(continued)

for another use.) Mix well and season the smash with salt, pepper, and additional lemon juice to taste. Serve immediately.

Prime Picks: Any very ripe tomato is a *smashingly* good candidate. The riper they are, the more liquid you may have to pour off as the tomatoes macerate. Consider it a tomato-water bonus.

Best left on the vine: Less juicy varieties such as Roma-types or paste.

Leftover Smash Salad Place 3 cups of cooked quinoa in a large bowl. Drain any accumulated juices from 1½ cups Mediterranean Smash and discard. Add the drained smash to a bowl with a small handful of chopped parsley (about ¼ cup), and 1 tablespoon each of extra-virgin olive oil and lemon juice. Mix well and gently fold in ½ cup crumbled feta. Season with salt, pepper, and additional lemon juice to taste.

Stone Fruit and Tomato Gazpacho

Makes 8 servings (about 7 cups)

I am a *big* fan of gazpacho in all forms. Late peaches ripen about the same time as backyard tomatoes and this is one of my favorite summer versions.

I always make a generous amount, but you can easily cut this recipe in half. I like to strain leftovers to use as a salsa-like topping on goat cheese and on sandwiches.

1 pound peaches or nectarines, peeled and cut into small chunks

1 large slicing cucumber or 3 small Persian cucumbers, peeled and cut into small chunks [note: slicers are what most large grocery store cucumbers are called]

½ medium red onion, roughly chopped

1 small jalapeño pepper, seeded and roughly chopped, or to taste

2 pounds juicy tomatoes, cut into chunks, plus 1 medium ripe tomato for serving

1 tablespoon extra-virgin olive oil, plus more for serving

1½ tablespoons cider vinegar

2 tablespoons freshly squeezed lime juice, more to taste

Kosher salt and freshly ground black pepper

6 lime wedges, for serving

2 tablespoons chopped basil or parsley, both if you have them

1. Place ¼ cup each of chopped peaches and cucumbers, 2 tablespoons red onion, and 1 teaspoon of jalapeño in a small bowl. Cover and refrigerate until ready to serve.

2. Place the 2 pounds of tomatoes, remaining peaches, cucumber, red onion, and jalapeño in a blender and puree until the gazpacho is as smooth as you'd like. (If you have a small blender, you may need to do this in batches.) Pour the gazpacho into a large bowl and add the olive oil, cider vinegar, lime juice, and ¾ teaspoon each of salt and pepper. Chill for at least two hours or overnight. Taste again after chilling and add additional lime juice, salt, and pepper to taste.

3. To serve, finely dice the reserved peaches, cucumbers, red onion, jalapeño, and remaining tomato. Add the basil or parsley (or both), mix to combine, and season with salt and pepper to taste. Ladle the chilled gazpacho into bowls, top with the tomato-peach salsa, and drizzle with olive oil.

Prime Picks: Juicy tomatoes such as Jaune Flamme, Red Boar, Missouri Pink Love Apple, or Chocolate Stripes are great here.

Best left on the vine: Paste or plum tomatoes.

❧ The Great Sauce and Paste Debate ❧

Every summer, some 'maniacs always tells me they wish they'd grown the "right" varieties to make tomato sauce. Here's the thing: I've yet to find a homegrown tomato that didn't taste fantastic in sauce and morph into a great homemade paste.

Commercial sauce and paste makers often grow the "right" varieties, but for all the wrong reasons. They're going for pounds, not flavor. That's why I toss *all types* of varieties into my sauce pot, from "cooking" varieties with few seeds and low water content to the juiciest slicers. You can always edit out the seeds if you prefer, but I encourage you to give them a try just once. Those seeds pack in a lot of extra flavor.

Tomato Sauce

Makes 4½ to 5 cups of sauce, plus 2 to 2½ cups of Top of the Pot Stock

"Seconds" (overripe or blemished fruit) work great in sauce and offer up a generous amount of Top of the Pot Stock (page 140) to use in other dishes. And when you are cooking a lot of tomatoes at once, skimming the stock off the top also cuts down on the simmering time. I like to keep the seasonings simple so I can spice things up in any direction later.

5 pounds very ripe tomatoes, any variety

½ medium onion

1 large carrot, peeled

2 large cloves garlic, peeled and lightly smashed

1 bay leaf

A sprig of thyme, if you have it

¼ cup extra-virgin olive oil

Kosher salt

Freshly ground black pepper, to taste

1. Smash the tomatoes with your hands over a large stock pot or Dutch oven, removing any rough spots and tough white cores as you work. Discard any skins that come off, but leaving a few is fine.

2. Add the onion, carrot, garlic, bay leaf, thyme, olive oil, and a generous pinch of salt. Bring the tomatoes to a boil, reduce the heat to medium, and cook for 20 minutes. The tomatoes will start to bubble pretty vigorously; just let them do their thing.

3. Use a ladle to skim off the translucent liquid that separates from the tomatoes (it's usually hanging out around the sides of the pot). Set the Top of the Pot stock aside and continue to cook the sauce for another 10 minutes.

4. Skim the sauce again, this time gently pushing down on the tomatoes on the surface to scoop up another generous cup or more of stock. Reduce the heat and simmer, stirring occasionally, until the sauce has thickened and is reduced by half, about 20 minutes.

5. Let the sauce cool completely and remove the onion, carrot, garlic, bay leaf, and thyme. Season to taste with salt and pepper. (If you are making paste, do not add additional salt.) If you prefer a smooth sauce, puree it in the blender. Use the sauce and stock within five days, or freeze.

Tomato Paste

Makes 1¼ to 1¾ cups

When I make paste in good crop years, I make an exception to my use-every-last-bit tomato rule. A few seeds are fine, but too many, and the paste can take on a slightly bitter flavor as they roast in the oven. You can use any variety of tomato, not just paste varieties.

1 recipe (about 4½ cups) Tomato Sauce (page 164), light on the salt

1 tablespoon extra-virgin olive oil

Kosher salt

1. Preheat the oven to 325°F. If the sauce has a lot of seeds, pass it through a food mill or press through a medium-mesh strainer to remove most of them. Puree the sauce in a blender until smooth.

2. Rub a large-rimmed aluminum baking sheet with the olive oil. Spread the tomato sauce evenly throughout the pan. Bake until the sauce begins to thicken, about 45 minutes, stirring with a heat-proof spatula every 15 minutes to redistribute the sauce along the edges toward the center so it doesn't burn. Rotate the pan front to back, and reduce the oven temperature to 250°F.

3. Continue to bake, stirring every 10 minutes to prevent the sauce from burning as it begins to caramelize around the edges of the pan. The paste is ready when the sauce has condensed to a thick paste and turns a rich auburn color (the shade will vary depending on the color of your tomatoes). This can take as few as 30 minutes or up to one hour, depending on the thickness of your sauce.

4. Store the paste in an airtight container in the refrigerator for up to one week. To freeze, spread the paste in a thin layer in a large freezer-safe bag so you can easily break off little chunks.

A Mid-Summer Night's Cherry Roast

------- - --- - ------ - - -- ⁔ *Makes about 2 cups* ⁔ --- --- - - ----- - ---- ---

The unsung heroes of the garden in my book? Cherry tomatoes. Many 'maniacs scrunch their noses when I suggest they grow cherries. Some say they have a "unique" taste. Others complain they had *way* too many cherries one year because they tend to grow like crazy. This is a problem?

If you're still not convinced, have you ever roasted a cherry variety? A generous pour of balsamic vinegar and a little brown sugar amplifies their natural sweetness like crazy. Sure, sometimes I overdo the sugar just a bit. Homegrown tomato candy? Still not seeing the problem here.

Great on their own, these tomatoes are also fantastic companions for homemade hummus, goat cheese, steamed green beans . . . I could go on. And by all means, play around with the vegetables and herb combos—and tomato varieties. This is a very pile-it-on friendly recipe.

2 pints (4 cups) cherry, grape, or other small tomatoes

¼ medium red onion, thinly sliced and roughly chopped (optional)

2 tablespoons extra-virgin olive oil

3 tablespoons balsamic vinegar

2 tablespoons brown sugar, packed

1 small sprig rosemary, cut in half, or 2 tablespoons mixed chopped garden herbs such as oregano, thyme, and basil

Kosher salt

Freshly ground black pepper

1. Preheat the oven to 400°F. If the tomatoes are large, slice them in half. On a large rimmed baking sheet, toss the tomatoes with the onion, if using. Sprinkle the olive oil, balsamic vinegar, and brown sugar over the tomato and onion mixture. Season with a generous pinch of salt and scatter the herbs on top.

2. Bake for 10 minutes and stir the tomatoes with a heat-proof spatula, mixing any stray pools of vinegar and tomato juice back together as much as possible. The juice from the tomatoes will help deglaze the baking sheet. Bits of vinegar will stick to the spatula; that's fine (when it cools, it turns into a handy "vinegar candy" snack for the cook). Reduce the oven temperature to 325°F.

(continued)

3. Continue to bake, stirring every 10 minutes, until the tomatoes begin to wrinkle but are still very juicy, 20 to 30 minutes, depending on the size, variety, and ripeness of the tomatoes.

4. Remove the tomatoes from the oven and transfer to a bowl to cool, scraping the baking sheet well, and season with additional salt and pepper to taste. Refrigerate for up to 1 week.

Prime Picks: Any cherry, grape, pear, or other small variety.

Best left on the vine: Any super-large tomatoes. They release water immediately as they bake so they won't caramelize well.

⩤ Back-Pocket Tomato Recipes ⩤

Recipes for those impromptu tomato days.

Tomato Cornbread

Southern friends, forgive me. There is not a drop of milk in this tomato-infused cornbread. If you like a chunkier cornbread, lightly sauté the kernels from an ear of corn and fold them into the batter.

Preheat the oven to 400°F. Lightly coat a 10-inch cast-iron skillet with butter or vegetable oil and place it in the oven. Mix together 1½ cups stone-ground cornmeal, ½ cup all-purpose flour, 1 teaspoon baking soda, and ½ teaspoon kosher salt in a large bowl. In another bowl, combine 2 beaten eggs with 2 cups room temperature Top of the Pot Stock (page 140) and 2 tablespoons of unsalted butter, melted. Lightly mix together the dry and wet ingredients (there should be a few lumps) and scrape the batter into the hot skillet. Bake until the corn-bread is lightly golden brown and a toothpick inserted in the center comes out clean, 22 to 25 minutes.

Tomato Gravy

A thick, rich, tomato-infused sauce for mashed potatoes, sautéed chicken, steamed summer veggies, and that cornbread, for sure.

Melt 4 tablespoons (½ stick) of unsalted butter in a medium saucepan over medium heat, add ½ minced onion, and sauté until the onions are lightly browned, 8 to 10 minutes. Whisk in 2 tablespoons all-purpose flour, cook for 2 to 3 minutes, until lightly golden brown, then slowly whisk in 1 cup Top of the Pot Stock (page 140). Continue to cook until the gravy has thickened, whisking occasionally, about 4 minutes. Season with salt and pepper to taste, and add a splash of cream, if you'd like.

Tomato Potato Gratin

Pasta marinara, meet scalloped potatoes. Vary up this impromptu gratin with fresh herbs, a layer of sautéed onions, or shredded cheese. Overly ripe "seconds" tomatoes work great here.

Preheat the oven to 375°F. Lightly coat a 9 x 13-inch casserole dish with olive oil. Peel and thinly slice 2½ pounds of russet potatoes (about 6 medium) and hand-smash 2 pounds of very ripe tomatoes. Drain the smashed tomatoes (reserve the tomato water), and fold in 2 cloves of minced garlic and 2 teaspoons dried oregano. Layer a third of the potatoes on the bottom of the casserole, sprinkle lightly with salt and freshly ground black pepper, and drizzle with olive oil (about 2 teaspoons). Scatter a third of the smashed tomatoes on top and sprinkle with freshly grated Parmesan (about 2 tablespoons). Repeat the layers two more times, ending with the tomatoes. Combine ½ cup tomato water and 1 cup heavy cream and pour the mixture over the potatoes. Sprinkle lightly with salt, pepper, and Parmesan. Cover the casserole with foil and bake until the potatoes are tender, about 1 hour. Uncover and bake until the top is beginning to brown, about 15 minutes. Cool 10 minutes before serving.

Seconds Strata

An anything-goes strata to use up leftovers. If you have homemade harissa, pesto, or hummus, slather it on the toasted bread slices, sauce side up, in the bottom of the pan.

Preheat the oven to 350°F. Lightly oil any size casserole dish. Toast or broil enough ½-inch slices of day-old, country-style bread such as Sam's Tomato Sourdough (page 173) to fit snugly in the bottom of the casserole. Drizzle the bread with olive oil (about 2 teaspoons per slice) and top with a 1-inch layer of leftover sautéed or roasted vegetables (a mix of onions, zucchini, eggplant, or whatever you have around). Lightly cover the vegetables with shredded, good-quality cheese such as Gruyère and top with a single layer of hand-smashed, very ripe tomatoes (drain the tomato water and reserve for another use). Sprinkle the tomatoes with salt and freshly ground black pepper, top with a small handful of chopped garden herbs, if you like (basil, parsley, a little oregano and thyme, or a mix), and another layer of cheese. Bake until the strata is lightly browned on top, about 40 minutes. Let cool for 15 minutes before serving.

Sam's Tomato Sourdough

Makes 2 large loaves

Full baking disclosure: I am not the baker of the family. Sam started making this incredible bread after our friend Scott, who happens to be a culinary school baking instructor, stopped by our house on his way to the Ventura County Fair. They made a sourdough starter together from grapes growing in our garden, and Sam has been putting Tartine Bakery's now famous no-knead rising and baking techniques to work ever since. Our BLT life has never been the same.

Our favorite variation was purely tomato grower's luck. After a particularly good growing season, we had *tons* of tomato sauce bubbling on the stove one weekend. Sam was making bread, so he substituted the flavorful Top of the Pot Stock from the sauce for the water. He's been making it that way ever since. And, in one of those full circle bread (and gardening) moments, he won first place at the Ventura County Fair for his Tomato Sourdough a few years back!

Note: The technique for this recipe was adapted from the *Tartine Bread* cookbook. The key, the bulk rise period, is all about getting to know your dough.

¾ cup (200 grams) sourdough starter, fed and ready to go

3 cups (24 ounces/700 grams) Top of the Pot Stock (page 140), warm but not hot (about 85°F)

6⅓ cups (850 grams) unbleached, all-purpose white flour

¾ cup (100 grams) whole wheat flour

1 cup (50 grams) wheat bran

2 tablespoons extra-virgin olive oil, more for rubbing your hands

1 tablespoon (20 grams) kosher salt

1. Place the starter into a large wood, plastic, or stainless steel bowl (do not use reactive metals like aluminum or copper). Whisk in the Top of the Pot Stock. Add the all-purpose white flour, whole wheat flour, and wheat bran and mix everything together with a wooden spoon or one hand until it resembles thick oatmeal (the dough is very wet, a good deal will stick to your fingers; try to return as much as possible back to the dough). Cover the bowl with a kitchen towel and set aside in a warm place to rest for 30 minutes.

2. Add the olive oil and salt to the dough, rub one hand lightly with oil, and use your oiled hand to mix the dough thoroughly. Loosely form the dough into a ball and transfer it to a large plastic tub with a lid. If you do not have a large plastic container, use a very large nonreactive bowl (wood or stainless steel) and cover it tightly with plastic wrap.

(continued)

173

3. Every 45 minutes, coat one hand lightly in water and reach into the container or bowl to "turn" the dough by grabbing under each corner, stretching, and folding it. Repeat with each of the round's four "corners." Re-cover and repeat the process every 30 to 45 minutes until the dough is twice its original mass and has a soft, almost fluffy texture, anywhere from 3 to 5 hours, depending on your room's temperature. If the day is cool, the process will take longer. If warm, the dough will come together more quickly. It is best to keep the dough in a warm place, free of drafts. (Sam puts his on the stereo cabinet where it is always 5 to 10 degrees warmer than the rest of the house—we listen to a *lot* of music.)

4. Turn the dough out onto a lightly floured surface and use a bench scraper to divide it in half. Allow each half to rest, covered, for 30 minutes.

5. Without punching down the dough, form each half into a boule, or round loaf, by pulling the sides of each down toward the bottom and pinching the seam together at the bottom. Rotate the dough as you work (cup the dough in your hands on the workspace) to form a ball, using as little flour as possible. The goal is to create some surface tension to form a better crust without deflating the dough.

6. Place each boule in a lightly floured, 8-inch proofing basket. If you don't have proofing baskets, line two 8- or 9-inch bowls with well-floured linen or tea towels. Allow the bread to slowly rise in the refrigerator for 8 to 12 hours or overnight, tightly covered with plastic wrap. (Or do as Sam does: Place the proofing baskets in a clean plastic trash bag, suck out as much air as possible, then seal the bag shut.)

(continued)

7. When ready to bake, preheat the oven to 500°F and place a heavy-bottomed Dutch oven or lidded stockpot in the oven. Remove the pot from the oven and carefully transfer 1 chilled boule to it (leave the second in the refrigerator). Slice across the top of the loaf 2 to 4 times with a sharp blade or razor, cover the Dutch oven with the lid, and return it to the oven. Immediately reduce the heat to 450°F and bake for 20 minutes. Remove the lid and continue to bake until the bread is dark brown on the bottom and golden brown on top, 15 to 20 minutes longer. Check the bottom of the loaf after 15 minutes to make sure it is not burning. The bread is ready when it sounds hollow when tapped. Cool the loaf completely on a wire rack before slicing. (Good luck with that. Sam and I can never wait that long.)

8. Return the oven to 500°F, reheat the Dutch oven, and repeat the process with the second boule.

New Tomatoes Rockefeller

Maybe it's lingering images of mushy 1950s-era stuffed tomatoes, but I have trouble convincing people to grow paste varieties like red and yellow Striped Caverns, one of the most prolific "stuffer" varieties I know. They're bell pepper–shaped, with sturdy walls, few seeds, drier flesh, and a cavity that can hold an impressive amount of filling. (You do have a few of these in your backyard right now, don't you?)

But by now, you probably also know what I am going to say next: *Any* tomatoes work well for stuffing. Super-firm paste varieties need a little longer in the oven than soft, ripe beefsteaks. The key is to avoid overbaking the tomatoes so they retain their shape.

This is essentially a baked salad-like take on Oysters Rockefeller, here with arugula and tossed in a super-lemony fennel vinaigrette. I like to make a big batch of croutons from Sam's leftover sourdough and keep them in the freezer for those impromptu New Orleans–like summer nights.

2 pounds ripe but firm tomatoes (about 5 medium)

1 cup day-old country-style bread such as Sam's Tomato Sourdough (page 173), diced into ¼-inch cubes

1 teaspoon fennel seeds

1 medium clove garlic, minced

1 medium bunch green onions, roughly chopped, including tender green stems (about ¾ cup)

¾ teaspoon Worcestershire sauce

(continued)

1. Preheat the oven to 400°F. Slice the tomatoes in half, length- or width-wise, to make little tomato "boats." Roma-style varieties tend to work well length-wise; beefsteaks width-wise, but it varies depending on the size and shape. If your tomatoes are too narrow to slice in half, slice the top third off of each. Scoop out the insides with a spoon and smash the flesh over a colander-lined bowl. Place the tomato halves upside down on paper towels to drain.

2. Place the cubed bread on a baking sheet and bake until lightly toasted, 5 to 6 minutes, stirring occasionally. Set aside to cool.

(continued)

1 tablespoon fresh lemon
juice

2 tablespoons extra-virgin
olive oil, more for drizzling

¼ teaspoon freshly ground
black pepper

4 cups baby arugula, loosely
packed (about 1 large bunch),
tough stems removed and
torn into 1-inch pieces

2 ounces well-chilled goat
cheese, crumbled

Kosher salt

3. Heat a small saucepan over medium-high heat and
toast the fennel seeds, shaking the pan occasionally,
until the seeds just begin to brown, about 2 minutes
(they will not darken significantly). Coarsely grind
the seeds in a mortar and pestle with a generous
pinch of salt. Add the garlic, 1 tablespoon chopped
green onions, and Worcestershire sauce and continue
to grind until you have a rough paste. Stir in the
lemon juice, olive oil, and pepper. Set the dressing
aside.

4. Lightly drizzle a 9- or 10-inch baking dish with olive
oil. Snugly arrange the tomatoes side-by-side, cut
side up, in the dish. Sprinkle the tomatoes lightly
with salt and bake until the flesh just begins to
soften, 5 to 6 minutes for juicy varieties such as beefsteaks, and 7 to 9 minutes for firmer varieties such as
paste tomatoes. Remove the tomatoes from the oven
and reduce the temperature to 350°F.

5. Meanwhile, combine the arugula, remaining green
onions, ½ cup drained tomato flesh (reserve the
tomato water for another use), toasted croutons, and
lemon-fennel dressing in a medium bowl. Mix well
and fold in all but 2 tablespoons of the goat cheese.
As soon as you remove the tomatoes from the oven,
divide the mixture evenly between them, packing
each tomato tightly with filling. Sprinkle the remaining goat cheese on top. Bake until tomatoes are
tender (but still hold their shape when pierced with
a sharp knife) and the arugula has wilted slightly, 5
to 10 minutes, depending on the size and variety of
tomato. Drizzle with olive oil, season with salt and
pepper to taste, and serve immediately.

Prime picks: Stuffers such as Striped Caverns, Yellow Stuffer, Liberty Bells, and Dad's Mug; paste or Roma varieties such as Enchantment, Polish Linguisa, Striped Roma, Opalka, or Big Mama. Beefsteaks and many other heirlooms also work well as long as they are not overly ripe.

Best left on the vine: Seconds or overly ripe tomatoes. The excess moisture can make the filling soggy.

'Maters and Grits with Garden Vegetables and Poached Mozzarella

Makes 4 servings

Those super-soft tomatoes on the kitchen counter, the ones begging to be tossed into *anything?* They're right at home in stone-ground grits. Yellow grits have a more intense corn flavor than white grits, but you can use either. (Okay, I'm nuts about grits of all kinds.) Any garden vegetables are fair game for tossing on top of the grits, though favas are especially good if you're lucky enough to have them. Poaching fresh mozzarella sounds like a high-end restaurant technique, but it takes all of five minutes—my kind of "fancy" cooking.

1 large ball fresh mozzarella, drained and quartered

1 large (about ½ pound) very ripe tomato, "seconds" work well

1 cup stone-ground grits

1 sprig thyme

1 clove garlic, smashed

½ teaspoon kosher salt

Generous pinch cayenne

Freshly ground black pepper

3 tablespoons extra-virgin olive oil, divided

½ small red onion, diced

1½ cups mixed garden vegetables, such as shelled favas, corn, and baby zucchini, sliced in half if large

½ cup small tomatoes, such as cherry or grape, sliced in half

¼ cup chopped parsley leaves

1. Preheat the oven to 300°F. Place the mozzarella on paper towels to drain.

2. Trim and core the tomato. Scoop out the seeds with your finger (leaving a few is fine). Place the tomato and 1 cup of water in a blender and puree until smooth. Add enough additional water to the tomato mixture to equal 4 cups (it will vary depending on the size of your tomato). Pour the tomato broth into a medium saucepan, bring to a simmer, and whisk in the grits. Reduce the heat to low and add the thyme, garlic, salt, and cayenne. Cook, stirring occasionally, until the grits have thickened, about 30 minutes. If the grits begin to look dry, add a few tablespoons of water. Remove the garlic and thyme, and season with salt and black pepper to taste.

3. Meanwhile, heat 2 tablespoons of olive oil over medium-high heat in a large sauté pan. Add the red onion and sauté until just beginning to soften, about 2 minutes. Add the garden vegetables and continue

(continued)

to cook until the vegetables are tender, 4 to 8 minutes, depending on the type and size of vegetables. Add the cherry tomatoes and any accumulated tomato juices. Sauté for another 2 minutes, scraping the pan to remove any brown bits. Immediately remove the vegetables from the heat and season with salt and black pepper to taste.

4. Just before serving, place the mozzarella in an ovenproof dish and toss with the remaining 1 tablespoon of olive oil. Place the dish in the oven, turn off the heat, and "poach" the mozzarella in the oil until it just begins to soften, 2 to 3 minutes.

5. Spoon the warm grits on serving plates, divide the vegetables among them, and nestle the poached mozzarella alongside. Sprinkle with the parsley and serve immediately.

Prime Picks: Any super ripe tomatoes work well in the grits. Green varieties will give the grits a more citrusy flavor, also good, just different. Same for the toppers—cherries and similar varieties look great.

Best left on the vine: Anything works in this recipe, just chop larger tomatoes.

Green Tomato Verde with Braised Chicken and Green Tomato Salsa

Makes 4 servings

In the fall, when the frost is threatening to make off with your last not-yet-ripe tomatoes, pick them like mad, then make this riff on pork chile verde. It's a great Sunday supper dish, chunky and stewlike and brimming with Swiss chard or whatever other fall greens you have on hand.

You can serve this over rice or slurp it straight up as a stew. Shred the chicken, and the leftovers make a great enchilada filling. If you luck into a bumper crop of end-of-season green tomatoes, freeze them, 2½ pounds to a bag, so they're ready to roll for green tomato verde throughout the winter. Vary the spiciness by reducing or increasing the amount of roasted chile peppers.

Note: If using frozen tomatoes, thaw them first and reserve any accumulated juices to pour into the stockpot. You can pulse the tomatoes in a food processor or puree them in a blender. The texture will be smoother, but frozen tomatoes release so much liquid, they can be tricky (and messy!) to chop.

2½ pounds unripe (green) tomatoes, blemishes removed and roughly chopped, divided

1 cup roasted, peeled, and seeded poblano, Anaheim, or Hatch peppers (6 to 7 small or 3 to 4 large)

½ bunch cilantro (about ½ cup, packed), leaves and tender stems, plus additional leaves for serving

2 pounds bone-in chicken thighs, skin removed and fat trimmed

¾ teaspoon kosher salt, plus extra for seasoning chicken

(continued)

1. In a blender or food processor, puree 1 large tomato, roasted peppers, cilantro, and 1 cup of water. Set aside.

2. Sprinkle the chicken generously with salt and black pepper. Heat the oil over medium-high heat in a large Dutch oven or heavy-bottomed stockpot. Add half the chicken and sauté on both sides, flipping once, until lightly browned, about 3 minutes per side. Transfer the chicken to a bowl and repeat with the remaining chicken. Set aside.

(continued)

1 teaspoon freshly ground
black pepper, divided

2 tablespoons extra-virgin
olive oil

1 large onion, chopped

2 teaspoons ground cumin

1 tablespoon dried oregano
leaves, preferably Mexican
(if using powder, reduce to 1
teaspoon)

4 cloves garlic, smashed

1 bunch Swiss chard,
spinach, or other greens,
ribs removed and roughly
chopped

Cooked rice, for serving
(optional)

Green tomato salsa
(page 188), for serving

Sour cream, for serving

3. Add the onion to the pot and sauté until just beginning to brown, about 4 minutes. Add the cumin and
oregano, stir for 30 seconds, then add the puréed
tomato pepper mixture, scraping up any brown
bits on the bottom of the pan. Add the remaining
chopped tomatoes, garlic, salt, and black pepper.
Return the chicken and any accumulated juices to
the pot (push the chicken down into the sauce so it is
well covered).

4. Cover the pot and simmer until the chicken is tender,
about 30 minutes. Add the greens and cook until just
tender, about 5 minutes. Season with additional salt
and black pepper to taste.

5. To serve, place one chicken thigh in each serving dish
with rice, if desired. Spoon the chile verde sauce over
the chicken and serve with the green tomato salsa,
sour cream, and reserved cilantro leaves.

GREEN TOMATO SALSA

Makes about 1¼ cups

Note: Frozen green tomatoes are too soft to chop up for salsa. If you're making this dish in the winter, substitute cucumbers or whatever other salsa-friendly veggies you have on hand.

1 large green tomato, on the softer side, chopped (about 1 cup)

¼ cup thinly sliced red onion, chopped

¼ to ½ jalapeño, seeded and finely diced

¼ cup cilantro leaves, chopped

Juice of ½ lime (or more to taste)

Kosher salt

Freshly ground black pepper

Combine the tomato, red onion, jalapeño, cilantro, and lime juice in a medium bowl. Season with salt, pepper, and additional lime juice to taste.

Prime Picks: Any tomato the day before that first fall or winter cold snap.

Tomato-logue

As the season wanes and leaves begin to fall, and you remove the last of the tomato plants from their comfy home in the garden, light a warm fire (or just brew a pot of tea, if you live somewhere eternally warm), and take a moment to recount your recent victories. It's been fun taking this journey with you.

Your triumph over hungry squirrels was epic, your win at the County Fair unparalleled, and your record-setting harvest, well, you (and the neighbors) will never forget it.

And then remind yourself: It's always tomato season!

Clean the garden from stem to stern, being especially careful to remove all tomato plant material and vestiges of last season. Then pile any newly fallen leaves on top of your tomato plot and cover it with a rich organic amendment. Add worms or worm castings, animal manures, and any other organic material you can get your hands on.

Now, you can rest and relax. Grab some catalogues and your garden journal. Jot down a few notes. Which varieties you loved, those you loved just a tiny bit less. Those that did well in your garden environment versus those that did even better. Next season, at least the planning part, starts now!

❧ Tomatopaedia ❧

Here are a few of the new, and yes, sometimes confusing, terms you will encounter as you grow America's favorite vegetable. Oh, sure, if you're the literal type, it's technically a fruit. We're always talking about these kinds of things on the Tomatomania Facebook page. Join us!

TOMATOES BY CLASS

Hybrid

A tomato variety bred to combine the desirable qualities found in the parent varieties, such as color, flavor, productivity, and disease resistance. Because the variety has not been stabilized, seed saved from a hybrid is not guaranteed to produce the same tomato if planted in future seasons. Today, hybrids often have the reputation that they are not as tasty as heirlooms, but when a) grown in your home garden, b) grown correctly, and c) picked when truly ripe, most will provide a thrilling tomato taste. Early Girl, Sweet 100, Beefsteak, and Sun Gold (one of the world's favorite tomatoes, by the way) are a few examples.

Heirloom

While there are several different kinds of heirloom classifications, the quality common to all heirloom varieties is that they are **open-pollinated** (some tomatoes might simply be marked OP). Properly saved seed from these plants will produce the same tomato in future seasons. Though some are modern, other heirlooms have been around for hundreds of years and handed down from generation to generation. Mortgage Lifter, Green Zebra, Black Krim, Polish Linguisa, and Giant Syrian are a few examples in this category.

Determinate (D or DET)

This tomato class produces fruit on the top, or terminal portion, of the main stem. When that happens, upward growth ceases, so this class of tomatoes tends to be smaller, tidier, and more compact. Determinates may not even need to be staked. Don't pinch too aggressively, as the side branching in this case will be productive, and you are working with a smaller plant. One reason people love them is that they tend to produce fruit in larger "sets" (meaning a larger percentage of the fruit on the plant will be ripe at the same time), which can be handy for making sauces and other tomato kitchen projects.

Indeterminate (I or IND)

Generally taller and rangier (as in, stretching all about) than determinates, the indeterminate tomato plant will not flower on the terminal or main stem, so it continues to grow. The plant produces fruit on side branching that grows off the main stem, providing steady harvests throughout your growing season. This is a bonus for snackers and salad-makers looking for a more measured, but steady, tomato supply.

Days, DTM, or Days to Maturity

The *approximate* number of days from planting to harvest. Key word: approximate. The numbers assume you are planting a six-week-old seedling, which is more or less the age of plants you find for sale in the spring. While certainly not an absolute, the "days" will help you develop your own strategy for planting, and then for early, midseason, and late-summer harvesting.

SOIL ADDITIVES AND ENRICHMENT

Amendments

Organic matter, soil, compost, and the like added to your garden area that increases bulk, nutritional value, and the soil's drainage potential. Tomatoes enjoy soil that is rich with organics, as most plants do. Amendments can be purchased in bags at your local nursery, but your homemade compost is always the perfect amendment (see chapter 1, Decomp 101, page 12). And remember to amend your vegetable garden all year long!

Mulch

Any material or materials added to, or laid on top of the soil around your plants to further insulate, protect, and aid in weed control. Hay, plastic sheeting, bark chips, and yesterday's newspaper can all be used as mulch.

Fertilizer

Food for your plants. You can choose to buy organic fertilizers or synthetic forms and I highly recommend the former. Organic fertilizers feed the soil, encourage the microorganisms there, and help develop the health and long-term vigor of your soil and garden. In granular, liquid, or pellet form, fertilizers provide the main nutrients needed for growth and fruit production: nitrogen (N), phosphorus (P), and potassium (K). Those represent the three numbers on the front of the fertilizer bags you just purchased. For tomatoes, look for a more balanced formulation. The numbers should be in the same range rather than very disparate. Fertilizer showing 30-0-0 is lawn food! The N-P-K indicators on organic fertilizers will generally be lower than on synthetic ones but don't fault them for that. That's just how it is.

PRUNING TERMS

Pinching

The (optional) act of thinning or "pruning" your tomato plants. Pinching involves removing new side growth from where it starts, just above where the leaf meets the stem. This thins the plant to let in more light, air circulation, and heat, makes it more manageable, and channels the plant's energy into fewer branches, usually resulting in larger fruit.

Left to their own (unpinched) devices, thicker, bushier plants will produce more fruit, but the fruit may tend to be smaller or less uniform. You won't want to pinch your determinate (DET) plants much—or at all (see DET/IND tomato classes above). Pinching is often a regional strategy. Cooler? Pinch more. In a hot spot? Pinch less; your plant and ripening fruit may need the cover. It's also a personal choice. Some people pinch religiously, others, like me, prefer not to pinch at all (learn more in chapter 5, page 90).

DISEASE CHALLENGES AND MANAGEMENT

Apologies in advance for making you sit through another high school science class!

V, F, VFNT etc.

V (verticillium wilt), F (fusarium wilt), N (root knot nematode), T (tobacco mosaic virus), and others. These degree-like letters on the labels of hybrids and some open-pollinated varieties offer clues to diseases or conditions that the plant will likely show some resistance against. If you are shopping online or from catalogs, your supplier should offer you a key for all these relevant notations to explain what each signifies.

Verticillium and Fusarium Wilt

Systemic diseases typical to certain planting regions or zones, and almost impossible to control. The entire plant is weakened (it will look wilted quite suddenly, often with yellowing leaves), and usually killed by the disease. These are soil-borne diseases, so remove that plant ASAP, and next season compost aggressively, and move your tomato garden if you can. Don't put that diseased plant in your compost pile. Get it entirely out of the garden.

Blossom End Rot

The tomato ripens with an often disgusting brown, bruise-like section on the blossom end, which is opposite the stem. Blossom end rot most often happens at the beginning of the season, before temperatures rise and plateau for the summer. Some varieties, Roma types in particular, seem to be especially susceptible. Long thought to be due to a calcium deficiency, it's pretty widely accepted today that early season stress (inconsistency in weather, water, fertilizing) is typically the cause. Add soil/horticultural calcium products, gypsum, or crushed egg shells to the garden every season, just to be sure. In general, mulch heavily, don't over fertilize, and water correctly to best prevent this situation.

Early and Late Blight

Early blight is exhibited by spotting/yellowing/defoliation of the leaves starting at the bottom of the plant and moving up the vine. It is best prevented by planting at wider intervals to allow more air circulation, and also careful water management. The plant can still produce fruit, but may be compromised. (But, a yellow leaf doesn't necessarily mean you have blight.)

Late blight is not curable (it was the scourge of East Coast gardeners in 2009 after a really wet spring and summer). It will not live through the winter in colder areas, but clean up the garden judiciously anyway! Follow the preventative measures mentioned above, stay vigilant, and remove any leaf that begins to show signs of disease. If you're growing potatoes in the garden, remove them, too. The disease is persistent in potato roots and tubers.

⁘ Resources ⁘

TOMATOMANIA!—The world's largest (and most fun) tomato seedling sale. For information on Tomatomania's new tomato trellis (see photographs pages 17 and 71), visit **www.tomatomania.com**

Want even more tomato info? Some favorites on our bookshelf:

You Bet Your Garden Guide to Growing Great Tomatoes, by Mike McGrath, 2002, 2009, 2012.

Roma-therapy, by Paul McCullough and Jeremy Stanford, 2013.

The Heirloom Tomato: From Garden to Table, by Amy Goldman, 2008.

100 Heirloom Tomatoes for the American Garden, by Carolyn J. Male, 1999.

If you're starting seed at home, look for some of our favorite seed sources:

WILD BOAR FARMS, **www.wildboarfarms.com**

RENEE'S GARDEN, **www.reneesgarden.com**

SEED SAVERS EXCHANGE, **www.seedsavers.org**

BAKER CREEK HEIRLOOM SEEDS, **www.rareseeds.com**

TOMATOFEST, **www.tomatofest.com**

VICTORY SEED COMPANY, **www.victoryseeds.com**

BURPEE SEED COMPANY, **www.burpee.com**

PARK SEED COMPANY, **www.parkseed.com**

HERITAGE TOMATO SEED, **www.heritagetomatoseed.com**

TERRITORIAL SEED COMPANY, **www.territorialseed.com**

Our friends at America's top garden magazines will always offer you great information on tomatoes and many other garden topics:

Fine Gardening: **www.finegardening.com**

Organic Gardening: **www.organicgardening.com**

Sunset: **www.sunset.com**

TOMATO-FRIENDLY ORGANIZATIONS:

For local and regional know-how be sure to make contact with your local arboretum, independent garden retailer, or garden shop and check out your local extension programs. The nationally funded programs do some great local work such as supporting the Master Gardeners program here in California.

USDA COOPERATIVE EXTENSION PROGRAMS, http://www.nifa.usda.gov/Extension/

AMERICAN SOCIETY FOR HORTICULTURAL SCIENCE, www.ashs.org

SLOW FOOD U.S.A., www.slowfoodusa.org

NATIONAL GARDENING ASSOCIATION, www.garden.org

❧ Acknowledgments ❧

Gary said, "Don't go back to school, come work with me," and then Sam said, "It's about time!" And so Hortus happened. In that era I rediscovered my affinity for, ok—obsession with, summer tomatoes. And then Susie Finesman said, "You should write a book!" And she took the bull by the horns and that's why this became a reality.

After twenty years in my new industry I was lucky enough to have Jenn Garbee harness my energies and help turn them into words. She channeled my story and all that I've learned and loved about tomatoes and she pushed, led, cooked, cajoled, and laughed with me through the process that ends with you holding this book. Staci Valentine and Valerie Aikman-Smith, Trude Rutan, Sam Hamann, you told that same story so well in the beautiful pictures that light up these pages.

I'm so grateful that after my lucky career and tomato flash point I had the good fortune to be mentored by Gary, David, Mark, Steve, Catherine, Kate, Tony, and all the now mythical Hortus team. How lucky that I landed in a business and a true community where customers became friends and taught me so much as they challenged me to solve their garden problems and find just the right ingredients for their garden environments.

We love being all about tomatoes, but inevitably every good and worthwhile endeavor is about people. I am endlessly indebted to Susan, Deb, Brian, Stephen, Laura, Fran, Steve, and all the 'maniacs who have sorted, toted, alphabetized, and championed these crazy and wonderful events as we grew to this point. It couldn't have happened without you.

My family, too, wears the 'maniac badge well! One of the nicest results of *Tomatomania* has been the opportunity to share our events and all this craziness with my parents, siblings, and extended family, whose support and love make it all so much more fun and meaningful.

And thanks to the kind and generous growers, experts, and friends who provide these jewels for us all to enjoy. Steve Goto, Brad Gates, Barbara and Bill Spencer of Windrose Farms, Jack Mayesh of Kobata Growers, and all the suppliers who nurture tiny seeds and turn them into these plants that delight us so. To Evan Kleiman and Slow Food Los Angeles, who pulled us through our transition years as we left the nest, and to all the hosts who have signed on to this crazy train at Tomatomania event sites, we couldn't—and wouldn't—do it without you.

Barry, Jonathan, Amanda, you've made us look so good and you have helped so crucially with the bigger picture. I'm lucky you dragged me into uncharted and utterly foreign territory. I really do like it!

It goes without saying that I'm hugely grateful for the guidance of BJ Berti and Courtney Littler and the generous and talented team at St. Martin's Press for their insightful and wonderful guidance in the development of this finished product.

This was such fun! If you're reading this book or this page and your heart is swelling with pride, accomplishment, or rich and meaningful memories, then I offer my most sincere thanks. You're why I'm here.

And Sam, there are not enough words, nor enough space.

COOGEE

❧ Index ❧

Page numbers in italics indicate photographs.